COURAGE
YOUR RIGHT HOOK

Martin Stark

Learn the Six Pillars of Courage, and Make Courage a Habit

Martin Stark

COURAGE

YOUR RIGHT HOOK

**Learn the Six pillars of Courage
and Make Courage a Habit**

About the author

Martin Stark, known as The Courage Champion, is a visionary entrepreneur, two-time LinkedIn Top Voice, and a globally recognised inspirational speaker. As a worldwide expert on courage, Martin's compelling narrative and groundbreaking achievements have captured the attention of prestigious media outlets worldwide, including CNN, CBS News, ABC, The Guardian, Out Magazine, and BBC World.

As the Founder and CEO of the World Gay Boxing Championships, Martin leads and influences global change in boxing and combat sports. His pioneering efforts to disrupt homophobia in boxing led to the successful delivery of the world's first boxing competitions for the LGBTQ+ community and allies, hosted in Australia and the United States.

Martin achieved a rare distinction as one of the few Australians to throw the ceremonial opening pitch at a Major League Baseball game, an event witnessed by over a million online spectators. With 15 years of experience as an IT Procurement Leader, Martin brings a wealth of commercial acumen to his endeavours. This blend of corporate expertise and personal triumph enables him to offer unique insights into resilience, leadership, and transformative change.

As a sought-after keynote speaker, Martin has delivered impactful presentations for industry leaders such as LinkedIn, TikTok, Transport New South Wales, Commonwealth Bank, and NRMA. His message resonates with diverse audiences, encouraging individuals, teams, and organisations to employ courage as a habit.

He was diagnosed with Addison's disease in 2006, shortly after having been placed in two induced comas and living through his worst fear – a tracheotomy. Having endured over 70 hospital admissions and four major surgeries, his near-death experiences have driven him to lead the positive changes he wants to see in the world.

Copyright © 2024 Martin Stark

All rights reserved. Thank you for purchasing an authorised edition of this book and for complying with copyright laws by not using any part of this book without prior written permission. This includes reproducing, storing in a retrieval system, and transmitting in any form or by any means, whether electronic, mechanical, photocopying, recording, scanning, or distributing.

I acknowledge the traditional custodians of the country throughout Australia and recognise their continuing connection to land, sea, and waters. I pay my respects to elders past, present, and future and to all First Nations people.

Legal Advice: Oceania Legal https://oceanialegal.com.au/
Editor: Christine Matheson-Green http://www.rememberpress.com
Designer: Gabrielle Sproat **www.linkedin.com/in/gabrielle-sproat/**

ISBN: 978-1-7637398-1-9

Some of the names of persons, organisations, and events mentioned in this book have been changed or fictionalised to protect the privacy of individuals and entities. Any resemblance to actual persons, living or dead, or actual events is purely coincidental and not intended to represent real individuals or occurrences.

Martin Stark

COURAGE

YOUR RIGHT HOOK

**Learn the Six pillars of Courage
and Make Courage a Habit**

Dedication

To George, you are my everything.

Contents

About the author iii

Dedication vii

Contents ix

Acknowledgements xi

Introduction xiii

Chapter One: Emotional Courage 1

Chapter Two: Physical Courage 19

Chapter Three: Moral Courage 37

Chapter Four: Empathetic Courage 57

Chapter Five: Steadfast Courage 77

Chapter Six: Cerebral Courage 95

Chapter Seven: A Place of Courage 115

Chapter Eight: Lean Into Fear 133

Chapter Nine: Commit to Values 151

Chapter Ten: Normalise Courage 171

Chapter Eleven: Be Consistent 193

Chapter Twelve: Courage Champion 215

From a Fan 228

Synopsis 230

Acknowledgements

A heartfelt thank you to everyone who helped, supported, and encouraged me on this journey. Your belief in me and this project has been nothing short of extraordinary.

When you have the courage to share your vision, people will help. They acknowledge your bravery and offer a hand up. The early stages of any project are often the most challenging, which is why I'm incredibly grateful to those who supported the World Gay Boxing Championships (WGBC) when it was just an idea. During these nascent stages, you often receive the best support to get your idea off the ground.

To Jenny, Sharon, Paul, Flavia – your early support as part of the WGBC board was invaluable in turning WGBC from a concept into reality. Special mentions go to Nick Bendel for creating the first WGBC website and Ben Baker for conducting the first podcast interview. I'm deeply grateful to Katie Neeves, Dr Joseph Nwoye, Celia Daniels, and Christine Granger for their invaluable guidance.

I also thank Charlie "The Hammer "Hall and the WBC for supporting WGBC from the beginning. I sincerely thank Denise Archie, Ivan Kaye, Ivan Schwartz, Mark Spinks, Mark Champley, Scott Hoskin, Peter Mousaferiadis, Kala Philip, and everyone from the Yarning Circle for their support and insights during those crucial early stages.

These individuals, among many others, provided the initial push that helped WGBC take flight. While I can't name everyone who contributed along the way (that would be a 200-page book in itself!), please know that your support, whether at the beginning or along the journey, means the world to me. You'll find additional thank yous throughout the book, acknowledging the many people who have played a part in this journey.

I owe a debt of gratitude to my editor, Christine Matheson-Green, whose expertise and guidance shaped this book. Thank you to Gabrielle Sproat for the striking cover design that perfectly captures the essence of courage.

A special thank you to Nicki Price, my publicist, whose efforts have been instrumental in bringing this book and my message to a wider audience.

The design theme of this book draws inspiration from amateur boxing, specifically the red and blue corners. These colours represent not just opposing sides in the ring but also the values inherent in the sport and in courage itself – determination, respect, and the willingness to face challenges head-on. I hope this design resonates with you and enhances your reading experience.

To my family and friends, your unwavering support has been my cornerstone throughout this process. Your encouragement kept me going when the task seemed insurmountable.

In the spirit of bravery and transparency, I'd like to acknowledge the use of AI in the research and grammar-checking phases of this book. This technology has been a valuable tool, and I'm grateful for its assistance. However, any remaining mistakes are entirely my own.

Finally, to you, the reader, thank you for picking up this book. Your courage in seeking growth and embracing challenges is admirable. I deeply appreciate your curiosity and the time you've invested in it. I hope it serves as a helpful companion on your journey.

Introduction

WHAT DO YOU DO AFTER WAKING UP FROM YOUR SECOND COMA?

I created the world's first gay boxing championships.

WHAT DO YOU SAY AFTER A TRACHEOTOMY REMOVES YOUR VOICE?

I spoke up and changed an entire sport.

Fear and courage are two sides of the same coin. I coined the phrase "Take ownership of fear, venturing forward with confidence and resilience." It's my definition of courage.

This book is my story of courage. It's about transforming the nightmares caused by the ordeal of surviving my worst fear and turning those nightmares into serendipitous dreams.

When faced with a dilemma, our choices are often made by the presence or absence of courage. If fear is the dominant emotion, we risk relinquishing control. Fear can also be an excellent source of information that bravely guides us to better decision-making.

Surrendering to fear is like living life with endless tosses of a coin.

Then, significant decisions are based purely on chance, or you outsource important choices to others to make on your behalf.

DO YOU CHOOSE COURAGE OR FEAR?

You decide when to be courageous and your cadence. I describe this as courage at your own pace. Here are the four steps to sustained bravery and greatness.

Courage at your own PACE: Four Steps

1. **PURPOSE:** Your inner fire is the catalyst that ignites courage and drives you to pursue something meaningful, achieve a goal or something you believe in. It's the fuel that motivates you to take the first step.

2. **ACTION:** Your steps of courage turn the dream into reality. It's about finding time and adjusting along the way, achieving progress by overcoming challenges and fear, and showing bravery in action.

3. **CONFIDENCE:** As you act, your confidence builds, and you improve. With each success, your confidence and capabilities grow, reinforcing your ability to face challenges. Action **instils confidence in you and inspires bravery in others.**

4. **EXCELLENCE:** The final step in the journey. Perseverance, consistency, grit, and confidently refining your skills lead to greatness. It keeps the pointless yearning for perfection at bay, enabling you to learn from mistakes, continuously improve, and celebrate success.

The coin toss happens before the start of every game of cricket. Two team captains meet on the field with the referee, and one captain tosses a coin while the other calls "heads" or "tails." This traditional ritual can significantly impact the outcome of the match. The winning captain must decide whether their team will bat or bowl first.

The choice made after the coin toss can be influenced by various factors, including pitch conditions and weather. The captain might decide to bat, take advantage of favourable weather, or bowl if the pitch is damp and likely to aid bowlers early on. The seemingly random act of tossing the coin can play a pivotal role – making the right decision.

As a closeted gay teenager living in 1980s UK, sport was a dichotomy. It was either an activity fuelling nightmares or pursuing dreams and achieving them. I was a county champion in competitive swimming but usually the last to be picked at school cricket. I feared the public humiliation of missing an easy catch and dreaded the tortuous ridicule of not hitting the ball when it was my turn to bat. It was utterly different in swimming. Friends congratulated me when I won medals in competitive events. Result? I captained the school swimming team.

The idiom "Batting for the other team" was a childhood paradox. People wanted me to bat for the other team because it increased their chances of winning the game. Most teams want to win. The idiom refers to someone who is perceived as being gay. 1980s Britain didn't like teenagers thinking it was OK to be gay. It wanted the exact opposite. This was abundantly clear in the social attitudes, prejudices, and behaviours. It was OK to treat gay people with contempt.

Decades later, the paradox is my purpose. My vision to inspire courage and disrupt homophobia in boxing is now a reality. Through publicly challenging homophobia in the hypermasculine, testosterone-pumping, and fabulous sport of boxing, I created a propinquity effect. This phenomenon refers to the physical or psychological proximity between people influencing the formation of relationships. Sport connects people and communities. It has a special bond where participants and fans cultivate relationships of togetherness and trust through their love of the sport.

In fear and courage, the propinquity effect plays a crucial role in how these emotions are experienced and managed. Boxing has a unique ability to enable individuals to confront and overcome fear. Training at a boxing gym for the first time can be like making new friends and being welcomed into a fraternity. The presence of supportive companions transforms the fear of striking the pads or sparring into an opportunity for courage. The shared experience and mutual support foster a sense of bravery, grit, and building resilience. The proximity to a bold and supportive crew converts trembling fingers into a fearless fist bump. Homophobia stigmatises a community. Removing the stigma strengthens and builds communities.

Muhammad Ali wisely said,

"Even the greatest was once a beginner; don't be afraid to take the first step."

CHAPTER ONE

EMOTIONAL COURAGE

CHAPTER ONE
Emotional Courage

DO YOU EVER REMOVE THE EMOTIONAL SAFETY BLANKET?

A warm comfy bed, is a haven on cold wintry mornings and a hindrance on hot, sticky summer nights. Quenching your thirst with a cool drink or putting the kettle on to make a hot coffee requires movement. You must get out of bed.

A safety blanket is made of material that burns slowly. It's a cover that stops flames from spreading or extinguishes them. Our minds can fan the flames of fear by allowing emotions to run wild instead of processing them with rational thinking.

We all need emotional safety. It's a cornerstone of a mind filled with enjoyment and not anguish.

Helene Brenner, Ph.D., and Larry Letich, LCSW-C described the three key points of emotional safety as:

- *A basic human need and an essential building block for all healthy human relationships.*
- *The visceral feeling of being accepted and embraced for who you truly are and what you feel and need.*
- *Feeling chronically emotionally unsafe causes intense psychological distress — and, often, greater isolation and more difficulty.*[1]

Emotional safety is a sanctuary, but humans need more than that to flourish. The world's most remarkable buildings started with solid foundations.

---

[1] Helene Brenner, Ph.D., and Larry Letich, LCSW-C "Emotional Safety: What It Is and Why It's Important" (Psychology Today January 16, 2023) https://www.psychologytoday.com/intl/blog/the-art-of-feeling/202301/emotional-safety-what-it-is-and-why-its-important

The incoming tide whisks away sandcastles where lighthouses withstand them. Safety can provide the building blocks of sustained growth and success or an island of missed opportunities.

Emotional courage transports safety to bravery.

WHAT IS EMOTIONAL COURAGE?

Emotional courage is the willingness to open up to a broad spectrum of emotions. You see what is possible beyond the walls of comfort, embracing new experiences with an open heart and mind. It's about being unafraid to feel deeply, to experience the full range of the unknown, and to take the essential first step.

Look at it this way: it's similar to an actor breaking the fourth wall at the theatre – that imaginary barrier between the stage and the audience. Frank Underwood frequently breaks the fourth wall in **House of Cards**, sharing his strategies and thoughts with us, adding layers of intrigue and depth to his character.

Emotional courage punches through walls of comfort. It enables you to manifest new opportunities and possibilities. It is you tossing the coin, choosing heads and delighted when it lands tails. (I tell people that's because that's what they want. If it landed heads up and they are quietly, mysteriously disappointed, then that's the sign that tails are what they wanted all along).

What happens next is not the fear of the unknown. It's the excitement of **discovery** and **character-building** through **experimentation and trying new experiences.**

Queen Elizabeth II's example

Queen Elizabeth brought the Latin phrase 'Annus Horribilis' into widespread use. It was how she described 1992, which saw the breakdown of royal marriages and Windsor Castle catching fire. Seeing her favourite home light up in flames while grappling with the tabloids reporting on every facet of Charles and Diana's separation must have been an emotional rollercoaster for the late Queen.

A rollercoaster chugs along rickety wooden frames that leave your stomach churning long after the ride finishes. Stoicism is the expectation of monarchy. Maintaining a stiff upper lip or "never complain, never explain" are masks for the public not to see how the late Queen truly felt. Uttering 'Annus Horribilis' was an excellent demonstration of emotional courage. It was a relatable expression of humanity after a tumultuous 12 months. It was her way of saying, "Wasn't that a fucking difficult year? We kept calm and carried on!" It resonates with Dr. Brené Brown's definition of moral courage: *"the ability to rumble with our story."*

MY EMOTIONAL ROLLERCOASTER

The Unexpected Battle for Life

The resplendent fireworks display lighting up Sydney Harbour signalled the arrival of 2006. What a cracking way to start the year! Deciding it was time for a new career journey, I resigned on the second working day of the year. After 8 1/2 years at the same company, it was time for a new challenge. 31 years old and a highly skilled professional with extensive experience in the telecommunications and IT industry. There are many opportunities out there. Five gym sessions a week, never smoking or consuming drugs, and rarely drinking alcohol kept me in tip-top condition. There was much to look forward to and opportunities on the horizon. 2006 was to be my year of differentiation. Life was going to change for the better...

A family trip to the UK took an unexpected turn. What started as a "sicky bug" was much more severe. Before I knew it, I was flat on my back in Grimsby Hospital's emergency department, a doctor looming over me with a grim expression. "Gallstones," he said, "blocking your liver."

How can this be happening? Older people have problems with their gallbladders. I'm young and healthy and can't have acute problems with my liver. But it was. And it was about to get a whole lot worse.

COURAGE

The doctors recommended a procedure to relieve the liver blockage. Like all medical procedures, it was considered safe but carried risks. Unfortunately, I experienced complications as dye seeped into my pancreas, causing severe acute pancreatitis and collapsed lungs. My next memory is speaking with a specialist in the Intensive Care Unit (ICU), struggling to breathe and fighting for my life. Every breath seems more complicated than Thomas the Tank Engine pulling twenty heavy trucks up Mt. Everest. There **are** no brakes, and he can't stop.

Acceptance over False Denial

ICU was a different beast altogether. More staff than patients, the air thick with urgency. A 40-something anaesthetist approached – his kind smile, a beacon in the sterile chaos. He had an impeccable bedside manner with a voice both tender and kind, and his words delivered with the utmost clarity.

The words clawed their way out of my throat. "I think... I need to go on a ventilator." His response was gentle but firm. "When patients ask for a ventilator, they usually need it. You need it."

Reality crashed down. This wasn't just a bad day – this was life or death.

You never know what you would do in an extreme moment until the moment arrives.

Acceptance over fear – and courage over panic – were my choices. It was better to be brave in what might be my final waking moment than waste precious minutes screaming in desperation.

Drugs used in induced comas are designed to suppress brain activity, leading to a state of deep unconsciousness. However, this suppression can interfere with the brain's ability to form and store new memories, often resulting in memory gaps or confusion about events during and around the coma. I experienced vivid and disturbing dreams, hallucinations, causing a sense of disorientation and difficulty distinguishing between reality and my brain's imagination.

My ICU memories are precious. They are my way of owning this most traumatic experience, controlling my narrative and sharing my story.

I was on a ventilator for about a week. Dreams, which were like living nightmares, caused PTSD. My mind created a fictional reality. Objects or people would feature prominently in the dreams. Some resembled sinister characters in old horror movies. Music played as I was extubated from the ventilator. The music is complex to describe, but it freezes my body whenever I hear something that reminds me of it.

Waking up from the first coma was horrific. My mind, untethered from reality, conjured up horrors that would make Stephen King squirm. The world was a blur of tubes and beeping machines when I finally surfaced.

A nurse's face swam into focus, her voice cutting through the fog. "You're in the ICU," she explained, each word a lifeline. "You've been in a coma."The tubes in my neck and arms and one in my nose feeding me made it almost impossible to utter a few words. Another nurse could lip-read. I moved my lips, and she understood what I was saying. **At last, a proper conversation. At a time of extreme torment, communication was calming.**

Surviving my Worst Fear

What would you do if experiencing your worst fear saved your life?

The thought of having a tracheotomy had always terrified me. Even writing about it now gives me shivers. While recovering from pancreatitis, I developed a severe infection that led to sepsis and the most extreme form of septic shock. This condition can rapidly lead to organ failure and death. Breathing now felt like Thomas the Tank Engine again, but this time pulling 50 trucks up the entire Himalayan range. I dreaded the idea of being put back on the ventilator, launching again all the nightmares.

Getting a tracheotomy was my only option.

The surgeon informed me he was going to perform the procedure. Sedated and immobilised, it felt like a python coiling its body around my legs, stomach, arms and chest. It holds you tightly, forming a safety blanket, helping you get through a delicate and intricate operation. The distraction from the fear was focused on the courage of the doctors and nurses performing the procedure; **their brave presence was a beacon of hope in the darkness.** Sensing their positive energy diminished the impact of the feeling in my throat. The pressure on my neck was intense. I was placed on a ventilator for the second time. The dreams were more disturbing and traumatic, but I *survived.*

Recovery and Renewal

Waking up from my second coma was a different ordeal. I was more alert and realised the gravity of the experience. My family was told several times that I would not survive the night. Ironically, they went to sleep, not knowing if I would be alive in the morning. I went to sleep twice, not knowing if I would wake up. Understanding the emotional and psychological toll this had taken on them **made the experience more relatable**. We had unique stories, making processing what had occurred and the road to recovery less challenging. **Talking helps!**

After a few days, a nurse removed the tracheotomy tube. Pressing down on my throat to speak, the voice wasn't me. The tracheotomy had damaged my vocal cords, and I sounded like a frog finishing an 18-hour shift at a smelting furnace. The staff encouraged me to start drinking fluids and sipping a smidgen of water through a tiny straw, which felt like a hose pipe extinguishing a fire in my mouth. It was as uncomfortable as eating a spicy curry when you have tonsillitis.

But, I discovered that nourishment of the mind revitalised my body and spirit.

Twenty kilos lighter and with little energy to walk, my new voice was croaky. It didn't sound like Martin; it was more like a polite Dalek from Dr Who. Spending time with my family and friends was the best medicine. Listening and sharing moments of laughter and joy brought healing and a stronger foundation.

My taste buds returned, making it easier to enjoy eating and gaining weight. I started going for walks and taking more steps week after week. The recovery initiated a new normal. Things would not be the same, but a new path in life was ahead. Six weeks after leaving ICU, I was back home in Australia and soon strong enough to do cycle classes at the gym. Exercise prepared me **mentally and physically for the major surgery I would need.**

WHAT CAN WE LEARN FROM ICU NURSES

How do they cope?

Nurses working in the ICU encounter significant emotional challenges daily, making their coping strategies crucial, for maintaining their own well-being while still delivering quality care. They are resilient and have strong emotional fortitude. They appear to keep their compassion and professionalism while working in a high-stress environment, constantly navigating emotionally charged situations.

But how?

From my ICU experience, I can say that the nurses' unwavering empathy amid potentially traumatic situations is genuinely exceptional. Despite witnessing pain and suffering, they consistently maintained emotional openness and kindness. It would have been easier to distance themselves. They stepped out of their comfort zones to connect. This willingness to be vulnerable and open-hearted became a **source of strength and comfort** for my family and me.

But at the same time, they're human. ICU nurses are not immune to the emotional impact of their work.

Like everyone, they can experience burnout, which is widely believed to be a state of emotional, mental, and often physical exhaustion brought on by prolonged or repeated stress.

In October 2018, nursing.org reported the critical symptoms of ICU nurse burnout are:

- *Emotional exhaustion is the single highest predictor of burnout, and depersonalisation is a coping mechanism we develop to deal with it.*
- *Depersonalisation from becoming so emotionally exhausted that they must "depersonalise" or become numb to emotion to protect themselves.*
- *Lack of personal accomplishment is frequently found in ICU settings where nurses often experience death, trauma, and arguably futile care.*[2]

Critical care nurses frequently prioritise self-care, which can involve focusing on **psychological, personal, and physical health.**

Jennifer A. O'Neill, chief nursing officer at the Hospital for Special Surgery, states that self-care must not be considered a luxury but a necessity. O'Neill engages in several activities to maintain a routine of self-care as a nurse:

- *Scheduling workouts three days a week and walking 10,000 steps a day.*
- *Carving out downtime to disconnect from technology and be truly present with family and friends.*[3]
- *Engaging in activities that give energy and enjoyment, including hiking and travelling.*

How can you Learn from their Example?

Leveraging emotional courage to increase the impact of our work is a powerful way to enhance your professional effectiveness and personal well-being. You can develop emotional fortitude by drawing inspiration

---

[2] Nursing Org Staff: Nurse Burnout Is Real: 7 Risk Factors And The Top 3 Symptoms (October 2, 2018) https://nurse.org/articles/risks-for-nurse-burnout-symptoms/

[3] Daniel Bal "Self-Care for Nurses" (Nurse Journal March 23, 2023) https://nursejournal.org/resources/self-care-for-nurses/

from ICU nurses' resilience and coping strategies. You may operate in a high-stakes environment. Our brains don't have inbuilt safety blankets. **No one is impervious to stress or difficult emotions.**

You can develop the grit and determination to challenges head-on, performing at a high level without carrying emotional baggage. This 'superhuman' resilience is built through self-awareness, **intentional self-care**, support systems, and mindfulness practices.

Here are six practical ways you can do this:

1. **Cultivate self-awareness:** Regularly check in with your emotional state. This awareness allows you to address issues before they escalate, maintaining your emotional well-being and effectiveness.

2. **Prioritise self-care:** View self-care as a necessity, not a luxury. This might involve setting aside time for physical exercise, disconnecting from technology, or engaging in activities that energise us.

3. **Develop emotional compartmentalisation:** Learn to create boundaries and prevent emotional exhaustion. This skill allows you to be fully present in your professional roles without letting work stress overwhelm your personal and home lives. Setting up a 'wind-down' routine after finishing work sets you up for a relaxing home time.

4. **Foster a supportive network:** Cultivate relationships with colleagues who understand your challenges. Regular check-ins or informal support groups can provide a safe space to process difficult emotions and share coping strategies.

5. **Practice mindfulness:** Mindfulness techniques can help you stay grounded in high-stress situations. Regular mindfulness practice can improve your emotional regulation and resilience.

6. **Seek professional help when needed:** Recognising when you need external support is a sign of strength, not weakness. You can be open to professional help when facing persistent emotional challenges.

We must take care of ourselves to take care of others.

EMOTIONAL COURAGE IN ACTION

While I was in induced comas, my mind was filled with vivid hallucinations and unbridled imagination. The powerful drugs and my suppressed conscious state created a surreal inner world, where fantasy blurred reality beyond recognition. These experiences offer a unique insight into how our minds grapple with the unknown and process extreme situations. Emotional courage helps in framing. It puts things into **perspective and prepares for the unknown**. Emotional courage becomes vital for maintaining sanity and finding meaning when faced with these confusing and often frightening mental scenarios. It allows us to frame even the most bizarre and unsettling experiences as part of our journey rather than as threats to our identity or sanity. It gives us the strength to acknowledge these experiences without being overwhelmed. I decided these hallucinations were part of my medical treatment rather than a permanent alteration of my reality. **Doing that helped bring healing and closure**.

Exercise: The Unexplained Journey

OBJECTIVE: *Transforming Challenges through Brave Thinking*

This exercise aims to develop your emotional courage and resilience by:

1. Exploring your reactions to an intense imaginary scenario.
2. Learning to reframe complex, challenging situations into manageable tasks.
3. Applying the Courage framework to real-life scenarios at Your Own PACE.
4. Practising self-reflection and emotional awareness in the face of adversity.
5. Developing strategies to overcome personal fears and obstacles.
6. Building confidence in your ability to handle unexpected challenges.

By the end of this exercise, you'll have practical tools to approach difficult situations with greater emotional courage, a more positive mindset, and improved problem-solving skills.

Imaginary Scene

Scores of excited families are waiting for a convoy of buses to take them to a theme park. Just as you give up all hope that the buses will turn up, you hear the drivers toot in unison. All the seats are taken five minutes later, and the buses exit the car park. Fifteen minutes later, there are roadworks.

This journey is no longer about going to the theme but one of survival. Your driver must detour along an icy mountainous road, which is dangerous and requires you to leave the bus. Walking slowly, you meander along the winding scenic path, arriving at a suspension bridge. It's 200m long and spans a 50m chasm at more than a mile in elevation – your safety hinges on your bravery.

A blizzard suddenly blocks the bridge's 360-degree panoramic views. As you traverse the bridge, the whip of the wind loosens the rivets. The safety railings on the side are hazardous as hissing cobras are holding on for dear life, blaming you for their predicament. The bridge swings rapidly and aggressively. Its reinforced steel was not designed for these weather extremities. You walk on and somehow reach the other side. It was a miracle you survived.

Reflection Questions

1. How does this intense scenario make you feel? Can you identify the emotions that arise as you imagine yourself in this situation?

2. Consider how emotional courage might help you in this scenario. How could facing your fears and pushing through discomfort change your experience of this journey?

3. Think about a time when you've faced a challenging situation in your own life. How did emotional courage help you overcome it?

Courage at Your Own PACE: Four Steps

Here's a reminder of the PACE framework.

1. **PURPOSE:** Your inner fire is the catalyst that ignites courage and drives you to pursue something meaningful, achieve a goal or something you believe in. It's the fuel that motivates you to take the first step.

2. **ACTION:** Your steps of courage turn the dream into reality. It's about finding time and adjusting along the way, achieving progress by overcoming challenges and fear, and showing bravery in action.

3. **CONFIDENCE:** As you act, your confidence builds, and you improve. With each success, your confidence and capabilities grow, reinforcing your ability to face challenges. It instils confidence in you and inspires bravery in others.

4. **EXCELLENCE:** The final step in the journey. Perseverance, consistency, grit, and confidently refining your skills lead to greatness. It keeps the pointless yearning for perfection at bay, enabling you to learn from mistakes, continuously improve, and celebrate success.

Applying the PACE Framework: Two Scenarios

Now that you understand the Courage at Your Own PACE framework let's apply it to real-life situations. Below are two scenarios to help you practice using emotional courage to transform challenges.

Scenario 1 is an example that demonstrates how to apply the PACE framework to a common frustrating situation. Observe how each framework step addresses the challenge as you read through it. This example will give you a model for applying the PACE framework in your own life.

Scenario 2 is for you to complete. It presents a series of questions for each step of the PACE framework, allowing you to apply the concepts to a personal fear or challenge. Take your time with this scenario, reflecting deeply on each question and writing down your thoughts. Remember,

Emotional Courage

there are no right or wrong answers – the goal is to explore your emotions, motivations, and potential for growth.

By working through these scenarios, you'll gain practical experience in using the PACE framework and develop your ability to approach difficulties with emotional courage. Let's begin!!

Scenario 1: A bus breaks down, causing you to be late for an appointment

1. **PURPOSE:** Recognise your inner drive to honour your commitments and maintain professional relationships. Let this motivation fuel your courage to handle the situation effectively.

2. **ACTION:** Take immediate steps to address the situation. Contact the person you're meeting to explain the delay. If possible, look for alternative transportation options or – even better – ways to conduct the meeting remotely. You might just be seen in the context of a solution seeker, which is a big tick in the business world.

3. **CONFIDENCE:** As you handle the situation calmly and professionally, notice how your confidence grows. Each problem-solving action you take reinforces your ability to manage unexpected challenges.

4. **EXCELLENCE**: Reflect on how you handled the situation and identify areas for improvement. Perhaps you could have a backup plan for transportation or leave earlier for appointments.

Use this experience to refine your approach to similar situations in the future.

Emotions can negatively impact your responses and results. Maintaining courage helps vanquish the brain's 'fight or flight' instinct and responses.

Scenario 2: Overcoming a fear of heights

Answer the following questions to apply the PACE framework to your situation:

COURAGE

1. **PURPOSE**:

- What specific fear related to heights are you facing?
- Why is overcoming this fear important to you?
- What opportunities or experiences might become available if you overcome this fear?

2. **ACTION:**

- What small, manageable step could you take today to begin facing your fear of heights?
- How can you gradually increase the challenge level as you become more comfortable?
- How will you hold yourself accountable for taking regular action?

3. **CONFIDENCE:**

- After taking your first step, how did you feel?
- What positive self-talk can you use to reinforce your progress?
- In what ways do you notice your confidence growing as you face your fear?

4. **EXCELLENCE**:

- What long-term goal can you set for yourself regarding your fear of heights?
- How can you use setbacks or moments of anxiety as learning opportunities?
- How might overcoming this fear contribute to your personal growth in other areas of life?

Remember to approach these questions with honesty and self-compassion. Your journey is unique, and every step forward is progress, no matter how small.

WRAP UP

Emotional courage isn't about being fearless but acknowledging and moving forward despite our fears. It's the willingness to be vulnerable, to face difficult emotions, and to step into the unknown. Whether overcoming personal challenges or pursuing our passions, emotional courage empowers us to live more authentically.

By embracing this journey of emotional courage, we transform our lives and **inspire and uplift those around us**. So, take that first step and embrace the process. Watch as your emotional courage grows. It opens doors to new possibilities and a more fulfilling life.

My three key learnings:

1. Emotional courage involves facing difficult emotions and embracing vulnerability to achieve personal growth.

2. ICU nurses exemplify emotional courage, offering valuable strategies for resilience in high-stress environments.

3. Reframing challenges as opportunities for growth can transform our response to adversity.

What are your three learnings?

CHAPTER TWO

PHYSICAL COURAGE

CHAPTER TWO
Physical Courage

DO YOU PREFER A SHARP SCRATCH OR A SLOWER, MORE ARDUOUS FORM OF TREATMENT?

Injecting medication into a vein gives it the most direct route to your bloodstream, providing your body with the most rapid access to medical treatment. Swallowing tablets or placing a dissolvable capsule under your tongue means it must be absorbed before the medication enters the bloodstream. An injection is usually the most suitable treatment and less arduous on your body.

Trypanophobia is the intense fear of needles. The overwhelming fright of a minuscule sharp object not much bigger than a pin causes many to trip out. It's estimated that half of all teenagers and about a quarter of adults are scared of needles. This fear can prolong pain and exacerbate illness. A severe fear can lead to missing doctor appointments or not adhering to prescribed treatments.

Elizabeth McMahon Ph.D. advised the critical points for overcoming the fear of needles include:

- *Identify specific fears and get the facts. Correct any misinformation.*
- *Plan for realistic, likely problems. Prepare in advance.*
- *Act on the facts, not your fear, and then praise and reward yourself for following your plan.*[4]

Doctors often reassure patients with the words, "Just a sharp scratch" when inserting a cannula. The procedure is usually over in a flash. After a

---

[4] Elizabeth McMahon Ph.D. "6 Steps to Overcome a Fear of Needles" (Psychology Today June 17 2023) https://www.psychologytoday.com/au/blog/overcoming-anxiety-and-panic/202306/6-steps-to-overcome-a-fear-of-needles

few moments of minor discomfort, the doctor's intervention can alleviate the pain of sickness, bringing a sense of relief.

Physical safety protects your health and well-being.

Physical courage is the difference between walking tentatively barefoot on a stony beach and running miles on one glistening with golden sand. It provides the groundwork for greatness and a springboard for success. Where fear stops some, this pillar of courage propels you forward, empowering you to take control of your health and well-being.

Muhammad Ali sensibly said,

"It isn't the mountains ahead to climb that wear you out; it's the pebble in your shoe."

WHAT IS PHYSICAL COURAGE?

Physical courage is acting bravely in the face of fear or pain. It's a transformative power that empowers us to face life's challenges head-on. It's the willingness to face physical challenges, discomfort, or danger. It involves being unafraid to feel physical discomfort, experiencing the full range of what your body can do, and taking that essential first step into the unknown. It transforms fear into strength, turning the unknown into an opportunity for bravery and resilience. It leapfrogs obstacles and barriers, supergluing them into the foundations of sustainable achievements.

Physical courage allows individuals to perform extraordinary feats, from a lifeguard diving into rough waters to save a swimmer to a bystander intervening in a dangerous situation or a healthcare worker treating patients during a pandemic. Physical courage enables people to protect others and achieve remarkable goals by conquering instinctual fears. Physical courage is a practical tool, a real-world version of 'Expelliarmus.' a spell from the famous Harry Potter series that disarms opponents. In this case, the opponent is fear. It is the key to **unlocking our potential** and **breaking down the barriers of fear and self-preservation.**

JFK's Example

President John F. Kennedy delivered one of the most famous speeches in history to an audience of 120,000. Glossophobia, the fear of public speaking, is a common fear. It's estimated that three-fourths of the population experience some degree of anxiety when speaking to a group of people. This type of social phobia causes discomfort and can lead to physical symptoms such as sweating, nausea, dry mouth, increased heart rate, and difficulty breathing. Delivering a keynote speech can be highly stressful.

JFK's "Ich bin ein Berliner" speech is a powerful demonstration of physical courage. The stakes of JFK's Berlin speech were monumental, occurring at the peak of the Cold War. His candid and forthright communication, a beacon of hope in a tense era, signalled confidence, authority, and an unwavering determination to resist subtle threats and subversive intimidation. Imagine the audience enveloped in an eerie silence. They hang on to every word of the speech. They absorb the diction, cadence, and strategic tone. Their positive response was a palpable relief for Kennedy, transforming the tense atmosphere into a peaceful one, akin to a refreshing breeze after a thunderstorm. Kennedy's physical presence and willingness to put himself in potential danger to deliver this message exemplifies how physical courage can inspire and transform not just individuals but entire nations. The historical context of the speech underscores its significance and the courage it took to deliver it, inspiring generations to come.

MY UNEXPECTED HEALTH BATTLE

The Presidential Disease

In August 2006, another battle tested my mettle in unimaginable ways. After surviving severe acute pancreatitis and two induced comas earlier that year, I underwent major surgery. This five-hour procedure involved removing my gallbladder through a large abdominal incision and repairing my bile duct. It was like a train being permanently rerouted along different tracks to reinstate a key commuter route blocked by a fallen tree.

If you can't remove the tree, you move around it.

After the surgery, there was an overwhelming sense of relief. The toxic tree from which Snow White's wicked stepmother picked the poisonous apple was no longer inside my liver. It was now a healthy orchard. There was no rotten apple spoiling the barrel. Unfortunately, there was a different barrel inside, one that would require even more bravery. I was discharged from the hospital a week later, but my recovery wasn't progressing as expected. The wound site became infected, necessitating readmission for cleaning. This pattern of discharge and readmission was repeated several times.

On my fourth hospital stay, fate intervened in the form of an astute doctor who noticed something others had missed. It was like a dog sniffing a single rose in a meadow of daffodils or a bat seeing a tiny orchid in a field of giant sunflowers. This observant doctor spotted a constellation of symptoms that had gone unnoticed. I had a slightly tanned look, shallow blood pressure that dropped further on standing, and blood tests showing low sodium and high potassium – all classic signs of Addison's disease. This rare condition, affecting only one in every 100,000 people, occurs when the adrenal glands don't produce enough of the crucial hormones cortisol and aldosterone. The doctor said, "Don't worry about the diagnosis; JFK had Addison's disease!"

Temporary Pain and a Lifelong Relationship

To confirm his suspicion, the doctor arranged for tests. These were far from pleasant experiences. Imagine getting a massive punch in one arm and three scorpion stings in the other. The first part of the test involved an injection in my left arm that felt like an instant knockout punch. This was followed by three blood tests on my right arm in less than an hour. My body, already weary from previous medical ordeals, protested vigorously, ramping up the pain receptors. Even the usually painless blood tests now had a sting in their tail.

Physical Courage

Turbulence is temporary. Fastening your seatbelts gets the passengers through the bumpy ride to the destination.

It was an eerie experience having a doctor investigate another medical issue after all I had been through. However, accepting the situation and drawing on the emotional courage from earlier health battles helped immensely. I was experiencing pain and fear, but acceptance gave me control. When the doctor confirmed Addison's diagnosis, an endocrinologist visited Dr Rory Clifton-Bligh. We hit it off immediately. He explained Addison's disease and what it would mean for my life going forward.

A healthy relationship fosters respect, vitality, and respect.

Like nurses, hospital doctors work long hours. The demands on their bodies and the pressure of diagnosing, treating, and saving patients' lives must have a significant psychological and physical toll. Doctors must have encyclopaedic knowledge and the mental fortitude to support patients who experience an array of emotional rollercoasters. Society has increasing expectations of doctors. How often do you ask your doctor, "How are you going?" While they focus on caring for us, who is looking after the doctors, nurses and all the healthcare staff?

Rory is not just my endocrinologist; he is my friend. His calm demeanour, wicked sense of humour, and ability to explain complex concepts keep my Addison's under control. I volunteer at the local hospital, helping Rory with education days for junior doctors who are training to become endocrinologists. We have collaborated on awareness campaigns.

What can you do to support your doctor?

Physical Listening

Living with Addison's disease requires a different kind of physical courage – the courage to listen to your body and act swiftly when something is wrong.

Cortisol, one of the hormones my body now struggles to produce, is like the essential fuel for a marathon runner. Just as a runner needs to stay energised to maintain performance and endurance, your body relies on cortisol to **keep functioning smoothly during times of stress.**

Imagine a plane that can refuel itself mid-flight, ensuring it can complete long journeys without needing to land. This self-refuelling is similar to the way cortisol provides the body with continuous support. It allows you to keep going without crashing. However, Addison's disease is like having only enough fuel for a one-hour flight when you need to travel from Sydney to London. Without sufficient cortisol, the body struggles to handle stress. Daily activities can become overwhelming, like a plane running out of fuel mid-journey.

Being knowledgeable about my new condition was crucial.

I learned this lesson just a few weeks after my diagnosis when feeling sick and dizzy, with lower abdominal pain and vomiting. Recognising these as symptoms of an adrenal crisis – a life-threatening medical situation required action. Physical courage now meant not ignoring these symptoms or trying to "tough it out" but seeking immediate medical help. I was quickly seen by a doctor who initiated intravenous fluids and hydrocortisone. It was precisely what was needed. Blood tests confirmed it was indeed an Addisonian crisis, likely triggered by an infection.

Day-to-day Physical Courage

Since that diagnosis in 2006, there have been over 70 hospital admissions. Each one has required physical courage – the courage to determine when my body needs help, seek that help promptly, and face the discomfort and disruption that each hospital stay brings. But physical courage isn't just about facing emergencies. It's also about managing a chronic condition day to day. For me, this means being vigilant about taking my medication, carefully controlling my stress levels, and being prepared for potential crises. It's about having the courage to explain my condition to others, **ask for help when needed**, and sometimes **say no to activities that might put my health at risk.**

WHAT CAN WE LEARN FROM ENDURANCE ATHLETES?

How can they embody Physical Courage

Endurance athletes demonstrate the purest form of physical courage. They push their bodies to the limit, testing human physical and mental endurance. These individuals showcase remarkable prowess, whether it's ultramarathon runners navigating rugged terrain or triathletes participating in Ironman events.

The courage of endurance athletes lies in their commitment to facing uncertainty and the unknown. The physical challenges, including extreme weather conditions, risk of injury, and fatigue, demand a high level of tenacity. Whether in ultra-marathons, long-distance cycling, or triathlons, these athletes willingly subject their bodies to prolonged physical stress, discomfort, and pain. This necessitates physical strength and an extraordinary level of mental fortitude. They endure the gruelling conditions and inevitable obstacles that arise during such events. They must possess the courage to persist when their bodies and minds are urging them to rest.

Endurance athletes are members of a thriving ecosystem supported by skilful coaches.

In March 2021, positivepsychology.com highlighted the crucial skills coached need to coach individuals or teams of athletes, including:

- *Ability to be nonjudgmental, understand people's responses, work under pressure and cope with stressful situations.*
- *Excellent verbal communication and interpersonal skills, patience, understanding, and the ability to motivate others.*
- *Problem-solving and decision-making skills, understanding and sensitivity.*[5]

---

[5] Jeremy Sutton, Ph.D. and scientifically reviewed by Amanda O'Bryan, Ph.D "14 Sports Psychology Techniques & Tips for Coaching Athletes" (Positivepsychology.com March 28 2021) https://positivepsychology.com/sports-psychology-techniques/

Endurance athletes focus on goals to succeed.

Sports psychologist and researcher Josie Perry wrote in the Sports Performance Bulletin about the four steps to focusing on goals:

1. Identify your outcome goal. If it is more than six months away, find a staging post where you can start working towards it immediately. Make sure you have direct control over being able to achieve it.

2. Decide on performance goals that show whether you are on track to hit your bigger goal.

3. Create process goals, which sit underneath each performance goal and are the specific actions you need to take to achieve it.

4. Review all your goals and make them SMART: Specific, Measurable, Accountable, Realistic, and Timed [6]

HOW CAN YOU LEARN FROM THEIR EXAMPLE?

Alex Honnold is the rock climber who made history by becoming the first person to free solo climb El Capitan in Yosemite National Park. This incredible feat involved scaling the 3,000-foot vertical rock formation without ropes or safety gear. Honnold's exceptional physical courage is evident not only in the climb itself but also in the years of preparation, his willingness to confront fear directly, and his ability to maintain perfect focus for hours on end.

You could have an exercise goal that involves "going the extra mile." The demands of your business or job could trigger stress and anxiety; physical courage can help reduce them. It replaces the fear of ambitious goals with a trusted spirit of dogged determination. Physical courage in endurance

---

[6] Endurance psychologist, Andrew Hamilton and Sports psychologist and researcher Josie Perry "When the going gets tough: 4 strategies to boost mental toughness" (Sports Performance Bulletin) https://www.sportsperformancebulletin.com/psychology/endurance-psychology/when-the-going-gets-tough-4-strategies-to-boost-mental-toughness

sports isn't just about extreme feats. It's also about the everyday individual who gets up to train, decides to swim their first 800 metres despite being out of shape, or continues to participate in sports despite a chronic health condition.

Here are six aspects of physical courage that endurance athletes embody:

1. **Preparation and Training:** Endurance athletes don't just show up on race day and hope for the best. They spend months, even years, preparing their bodies and minds for the challenges ahead.

2. **Mental Toughness:** Physical endurance is more about mental strength than physical capability. Athletes like Honnold demonstrate incredible mental toughness, pushing through the voice telling them to quit.

3. **Embracing Discomfort:** Endurance athletes don't shy away from discomfort; they lean into it. They understand that growth and achievement often lie on the other side of it.

4. **Risk Management**: While these athletes take on significant risks, they do so with calculated intent. They prepare meticulously, understand their limits, and make informed decisions about when to push, and when to pull back.

5. **Resilience in the Face of Setbacks:** Not every race or climb goes as planned. In fact, few do. Endurance athletes often face unexpected challenges, injuries, or failures. They bounce back from these setbacks and keep pushing towards their goals.

6. **Skills That Can Be Developed Over Time:** Physical courage is not a fixed trait. Through consistent effort, and a willingness to face your fears, you can cultivate more extraordinary physical courage in your life.

Incremental steps lead to excellent outcomes.

PHYSICAL COURAGE IN ACTION

Physical courage often manifests in overcoming deeply ingrained fears. I was terrified of snakes and sometimes had nightmares about a serpent biting me. Growing up in the UK, **my fear was primarily theoretical.** When I migrated to Australia, a country renowned for the most venomous snakes in the world, it was not exactly baseless. I avoided activities such as bushwalking in case I saw a snake.

In 2019, I visited Wildlife Sydney with a mission: to tell a snake I was his mate. Approaching Houdini, an olive python, my heart raced. The handler invited me to touch him – a moment of truth. I extended my hand and discovered Houdini's body felt like a firm, comfortable pillow, not the slimy texture I'd imagined. Houdini wrapped his body around my arm, replacing my fear with wonder and respect. He showed that reality often differs from our frightful imagination, which frequently works overtime.

The experience taught me that physical courage isn't just about feats of strength. It's about challenging our physical reactions to fear and putting ourselves in uncomfortable situations to grow. By facing my fear, I conquered a phobia and gained an appreciation for these creatures. When I think of snakes, I remember Houdini's **gentle nature, not fear.**

Exercise: The Physical Challenge

OBJECTIVE: *Embracing Challenges for Growth*

This exercise aims to develop your physical courage by:

1. Exploring your reactions to an intense physical challenge scenario.
2. Learning to reframe difficult physical situations into manageable tasks.
3. Applying physical courage concepts to real-life scenarios.
4. Practising self-reflection and body awareness in the face of physical adversity.
5. Developing strategies to overcome physical fears and obstacles.

6. Building confidence in your ability to handle unexpected physical challenges.

By the end of this exercise, you'll have practical tools to approach physically demanding situations with greater courage, a more positive mindset, and improved problem-solving skills.

Imaginary Scene

You're stranded in the Australian outback. Your four-wheel drive has run out of fuel, and you forgot to charge your mobile phones. The scorching sun beats down relentlessly, and the harsh, arid landscape stretches as far as the eye can see. Your water supply is depleted. A pub is 10 kilometres away, and you want to quench your thirst with a nice cold beer. There is a small convenience store and petrol station next to the pub.

You must embark on a long walk to find the pub. Every step is a battle against extreme heat, exhaustion, and the unforgiving terrain. There are lizards, scorpions, and spiders along the dirt road. Your survival depends entirely on your physical endurance, mental resilience, and courage to keep moving forward despite the odds. You finally make it to the pub five minutes before closing time. Your tongue is gasping for that beer. You check your pocket and realise you have left your wallet in the car. The kind Aussie barman buys you the beer!

Reflection Questions

1. How does this intense physical challenge scenario make you feel? Can you identify the emotions and physical sensations that arise as you imagine yourself in this situation?

2. Now, consider how physical courage might help you in this scenario. How could facing your physical limitations and pushing through discomfort change your experience of this journey?

3. Think about a time when you've faced a physically demanding situation in your own life. How did physical courage help you overcome it?

Applying Physical Courage: Two Scenarios

Now that you've considered the concept of physical courage through the outback scenario let's apply it to real-life situations using the PACE framework: Purpose, Action, Confidence, and Excellence. Below are two scenarios to help you practice using physical courage to transform challenges.

Scenario 1 is an example that demonstrates how to apply the PACE framework to a shared physical challenge. As you read through it, observe how each step of the framework addresses the challenge. This example will give you a model for applying PACE in your own life.

Scenario 2 is for you to complete. It presents a series of questions for each step of the PACE framework, allowing you to apply the concepts to a personal physical fear or challenge. Take your time with this scenario, reflecting deeply on each question and writing down your thoughts. Remember, there are no right or wrong answers – the goal is to explore your physical reactions, motivations, and growth potential.

By working through these scenarios, you'll gain practical experience in using the PACE framework to develop physical courage. Let's begin!

Scenario 1: Starting a new fitness routine

PURPOSE: Recognise your inner drive for better health and increased energy. Let this motivation fuel your courage to start and maintain a new fitness routine.

ACTION: Take immediate steps to begin your fitness journey. Research workout plans suitable for your fitness level or consider hiring a personal trainer. Set a specific schedule for your workouts and prepare your exercise gear.

CONFIDENCE: Acknowledge your progress as you complete each workout, no matter how small. Each step reinforces your ability to improve your physical fitness and face challenges.

EXCELLENCE: Reflect on your fitness journey and identify areas for improvement. Perhaps you could increase the intensity of your workouts or try new forms of exercise. Use this experience to refine your approach to fitness and overall health continually.

Scenario 2: Overcoming a fear of spiders

Answer the following questions to apply the PACE framework to your situation:

1. **PURPOSE:**

- What specific fear related to spiders are you facing?
- Why is overcoming this fear important to you?
- What opportunities or experiences might become available to you if you overcome this fear?

2. **ACTION:**

- What small, manageable step could you take today to begin facing your fear of spiders?
- How can you gradually increase the challenge level as you become more comfortable?
- How will you hold yourself accountable for taking regular action?

3. **CONFIDENCE:**

- After taking your first step, how did you feel physically and emotionally?
- What positive self-talk can you use to reinforce your progress?
- In what ways do you notice your confidence growing as you face your fear?

4. **EXCELLENCE:**

- What long-term goal can you set regarding your fear of spiders?

- How can you use setbacks or moments of anxiety as learning opportunities?
- How might overcoming this fear contribute to your personal growth in other areas of life?

Remember to approach these questions with honesty and self-compassion. Your journey of developing physical courage is unique, and every step forward, no matter how small, is progress.

WRAP UP

Physical courage isn't about invincibility but acknowledging and moving forward despite our physical limitations. It's the willingness to be vulnerable, to face physical discomfort, and to step into the unknown. Whether overcoming health challenges or pursuing athletic goals, physical courage empowers us to live with more vitality and impact.

Adopting physical courage is appreciated by your body and mind. They relish the nutritious energy you provide, bringing a warm smile to your face with an infectious spirit. Others want to **emulate your bravery**. You are **the coach successful people want in their corner.**

My three key learnings:

1. Physical courage is not about being fearless but acknowledging fears and physical limitations and pushing forward despite them.
2. Endurance athletes exemplify physical courage, which involves consistent preparation, mental toughness, and embracing discomfort for long-term goals.
3. Building physical courage is a gradual process that can be developed through small, everyday actions, from starting a new fitness routine to facing physical fears. I overcame my fear of spiders!

Physical Courage

What are your three learnings?

CHAPTER THREE

MORAL COURAGE

CHAPTER THREE
Moral Courage

HOW DOES YOUR MORAL COMPASS HELP YOU?

Morality is the guiding principle determining what is acceptable or unacceptable in society. We uphold specific values like respect, courtesy, dignity, and honesty. Your moral compass is your internal navigation system, helping you distinguish right and wrong. It's not static but adapts and evolves, influenced by personal experiences, knowledge, and challenges. Your moral compass is not set in stone; it adjusts as you encounter new situations that may challenge your beliefs and values.

Each day brings new ethical dilemmas, providing opportunities to refine and readjust your moral compass. No single day or decision defines it.

David Weitzner Ph.D. advised the essential components of trusting your moral compass in times of doubt and uncertainty include:

- *There is growing pressure to reframe undecidable dilemmas as complex problems that can be solved using algorithmic tools like advanced AI.*
- *When we exhaust our capacity for calculation, we turn to our internal moral compass for guidance on how to proceed.*
- *We need to reject the message encouraging us to doubt our natural capacities to do good and trust our cooperative intuitions.*[7]

Everyone's moral compass is unique. Even universally accepted moral concepts can manifest in diverse ways. This uniqueness underscores the

---

[7] David Weitzner Ph.D "The Danger in Not Trusting Our Moral Compass" (Psychology Today December 9, 2022) https://www.psychologytoday.com/au/blog/managing-with-meaning/202212/the-danger-in-not-trusting-our-moral-compass

importance of determining your path in the face of societal expectations and personal convictions.

Your moral compass allows you to act with integrity and solidifies your trustworthy reputation.

WHAT IS MORAL COURAGE?

Moral courage is taking a firm stand for what you believe in and committing to your values. It involves standing up for what is right, even when faced with opposition, criticism, or potential repercussions. This type of courage requires adhering to your principles and ethics, regardless of the consequences.

It's like a whistleblower exposing unethical practices in their organisation or someone speaking out against injustice in their community. Moral courage breaks through the walls of conformity and fear of social repercussions. It allows you to act with integrity and honour when others don't.

Moral courage is a transformative force for good. It's the activist fighting for human rights, the employee challenging discriminatory policies, or the friend defending someone being mistreated.

People with moral courage inspire change and foster justice by steadfastly holding to their values and beliefs.

Nelson Mandela's example

Nelson Mandela, the anti-apartheid revolutionary and former President of South Africa, exemplifies moral courage globally. His unwavering commitment to equality and justice in the face of extreme adversity inspires millions worldwide. Mandela's journey began as a young lawyer and activist, fighting against the oppressive apartheid system in South Africa. Despite the personal risks, he chose to stand up against racial segregation and discrimination. His moral courage was put to the ultimate test when he was arrested in 1962 and subsequently sentenced to life

Moral Courage

imprisonment. He served his sentence for his country. He sacrificed almost three decades of confinement for the future liberty of tens of millions.

During his 27 years in prison, he did not waver. He refused to compromise his principles in exchange for his freedom. Instead, he used his time to educate himself and his fellow prisoners, becoming a symbol of hope. Upon his release in 1990, Mandela demonstrated extraordinary leadership by advocating for reconciliation rather than revenge. He said, "As I walked out the door toward the gate that would lead to my freedom, I knew if I didn't leave my bitterness and hatred behind, I'd still be in prison." This commitment to forgiveness and unity was crucial to South Africa's transition to democracy. He worked tirelessly to heal the deep wounds of his nation's past. He established the Truth and Reconciliation Commission, a bold and innovative approach to addressing past human rights abuses. This is a shining example for other countries to adopt.

Mandela's life demonstrates that moral courage is not just about standing up for what's right in moments of crisis but maintaining that stance over a lifetime. His famous quote encapsulates this:

"I learned that courage was not the absence of fear, but the triumph over it. The brave man is not he who does not feel afraid, but he who conquers that fear."

MY JOURNEY TO BE ME

The Iron Lady Next Door

Margaret Thatcher could have been my neighbour. She came to power when I was fear years old – this is not a typo. I was four in 1979 and spent my formative years scared of who I was and the way society treated gay men with utter contempt. My journey with moral courage began in the small town of Grimsby, England, in the late 1970s and early 1980s. My maternal grandparents and mum lived in Grantham for a short time in the 1950s, just down the street from the Roberts family shop that Margaret Thatcher's parents owned. If my family had stayed in Grantham, Mrs T could have been the neighbour we called "Auntie Maggie."

We are all homo sapiens.

Growing up, I was acutely aware of the four crucial letters in the two words describing humans: Homo. All humans are Homo sapiens, as my school's trusty Encyclopaedia Britannica informed me. Yet, it was painful to understand why parts of humanity had such problems accepting homos like me. The prejudice and hatred towards people just wanting to be happy caused excessive pain, harm, and sometimes even death. Some politicians indoctrinated an unfounded fear that acceptance of gay people was the wrong thing to do. It inculcated an intense fear of accepting being me.

To understand the cultural climate of the time, you only need to watch popular British sitcoms of the 1980s. Gay men were often seen as parodies and objects of ridicule. For example, Lt. Gruber in "'Allo 'Allo" was a character that perpetuated these stereotypes. Ironically, while Guy Siner, the actor who played the effeminate Lt. Gruber, is straight, Gordon Kaye, who portrayed René, the café owner and object of Gruber's affection, was gay.

By the way, I love 'Allo 'Allo. It's hilarious.

We gays can laugh at ourselves and invite everyone to join us.

Storm Clouds and Silver Lining

The late 1980s was exceptionally challenging for the UK LGBTQ+ community. At The Conservative Party's annual conference, Margaret Thatcher said, "Children who need to be taught traditional moral values are being taught they have an inalienable right to be gay." She followed this up with "...children are being cheated of a sound start in life – yes cheated."

In 1988, the UK government introduced Section 28. This legislation prohibited local authorities from "promoting homosexuality" or teaching

Moral Courage

"the acceptability of homosexuality as a pretended family relationship." It prevented schools or councils from providing any support. This legislation sparked significant backlash and protest from gay activists and allies. The activists who **stood up** against this legislation **demonstrated true moral courage.**

Moral crusades are the antithesis of moral courage. The rhetoric and legalised discrimination against the LGBTQ+ community were the absolute pits. It incited fear in society about gay people, instilling fright into an 11, 12, 13, 14 and 15-year-old who struggled to accept he was gay.

Glimmers of hope and allyship.

Visible representation is crucial for removing stigma and breaking down barriers. Eastenders is a BBC soap opera with an audience surpassing 15 million in the 1980s. The entire nation talked about it. It featured Colin and Barry, one of the first openly gay couples on mainstream British television. It provided a rare glimpse and groundbreaking portrayal of gay men living normal lives. Colin and Barry were depicted with depth and humanity, navigating relationships' typical ups and downs. **They were just like other couples.**

On 17 November 1987, Colin kissed Barry on the forehead. What an outrage! Straight couples don't cause opprobrium when they kiss each other. Forehead GAYte ignited a media firestorm. It drew sharp criticism from conservative politicians. The tabloid newspaper The Sun ran a sensationalist headline, "EastBenders." Yet, despite the backlash, Colin and Barry's presence on EastEnders marked a fundamental step towards greater visibility and acceptance. Colin kissed his partner two years later, and the media barely mentioned it. **Progress had been made.**

I particularly admired June Brown, who played Dot Cotton. While her character was initially pious and judgmental, reflecting the prejudices of the time, June herself was an ardent supporter of the LGBTQ+ community. Her off-screen activism and public statements reflected her deep commitment to inclusion. Watching Dot's character evolve over the years, slowly beginning to see Colin and Barry not just as gay men but

COURAGE

as individuals deserving of respect and love, gave me **hope that society could change, too.**

Three Little Words

My first job after graduating was as a team manager at a British Telecom (BT) call centre in Grimsby. The workplace culture was a mix of acceptance and a soupçon of homophobia. My peers and the staff were kind and accepting. Some higher-ups, particularly my manager, were dinosaurs from a bygone era. My manager made it clear how he felt about gay people with his disparaging remarks and "jokes." I was even dubbed "The whipping boy," a scapegoat when things went wrong.

My mind was constantly weighing the risks of being myself against the safety of staying closeted. However, incremental steps gave me hope. When my manager sent me on a training course, it was an opportunity to visit a gay bar for the first time. The facilitator of the training course was gay and would later be a **mentor offering guidance and wisdom.**

Hiding was tortuous. Accepting who we are is easier than pretending to be someone else.

The turning point came with the new millennium. It was time for a change, and I called the BT office in Sydney, asking for a job. Leaving everything familiar, taking voluntary redundancy from BT in the UK and travelling to Australia on a working holiday visa was an exciting adventure.

The culture in the Sydney office was fantastic. My new colleagues, who quickly became friends, were fabulous. They spoke warmly about LGBTQ+ people, deriding homophobes and showing they were a passionate and caring crew. In this supportive environment, **I found the bravery to come out.**

At the age of 27, I plucked up the courage to call a relative and utter the three words that had been stuck in my throat for so long: **"I am gay!"** The response – **"I know, and we all love you"** – was overwhelmingly positive and affirming. This was not a surprise, but two decades of fear delayed me from sharing who I was. The experience was repeated with most of my family and friends. Those who didn't suspect I was gay just wanted me to be happy and enjoy life.

This journey taught me that moral courage isn't just about grand gestures or public stands. It's about the small, everyday decisions to be true to oneself and to stand up for what's right. It's about choosing authenticity over safety, even when uncomfortable or risky.

Coming Out to "Auntie Maggie"

I often wonder what life would have been like if our family had lived in my grandparents' old house in Grantham. Imagine Auntie Maggie dropping by for afternoon tea after her '1987 speech'.

She is arriving at 3 o'clock and can stay for 15 minutes. I quickly go to the corner shop and buy a whoopee cushion noticing the 'adult' magazines on the top shelf. This is "strategic knowledge" and a possible future deterrent to the eyes of thunder in an angry person.

Auntie Maggie always sits on the wooden kitchen chair with a scatter cushion. No one is looking. I blow up the whoopee cushion and place it under the scatter cushion. The scene is set! At 3 p.m., there are three knocks on the front door. Mum has the tea and cake ready. The dining room table is laid out with the best plates and a posh Royal Worcester tea set. I get the kitchen chair as the family goes to the front door. Auntie Maggie is polite and pleased to see us. She removes her blue coat and holds her blue handbag. She moseys in her blue shoes into the dining room, leaving the coat and bag on a red armchair.

Auntie Maggie sits down. The whoopee cushion lets one rip! It sounded like a fart that would empty a pub packed with thirsty coal miners after a 12-hour shift. Laughter erupts. She is angry with her eyes, communicating her ferocity.

As she opens her mouth, my uttering flummoxes her, "I'm gay, and you're a bully!" This is followed up with the killer line, "The gay is not for turning!"

COURAGE

Her shock turns to … the politician. She talks about family values and how hard life will be for me. She listens to my explaining that her attitude and bigotry are the things that make it difficult. I want to be accepted and not hated. I follow up by asking, "Why does your shop sell pornographic magazines? What about family values?" My older brother laughs at the potential tabloid headline: Maggie's Roast Beef and Lincolnshire Farting!" Auntie Maggie takes out a blue handkerchief from her handbag. She wipes a tear from her left eye. She apologises and promises to try better and understand. We all walk her to the front door, telling her she's always welcome.

If only!

> # Vocal Moment is a support site that helps people find their voices and speak up. It empowers you to become the change you wish to see as we equip you with the tools to speak up confidently and clearly. This transformative experience helps you shed shyness and regrets and embrace precise, effective communication that consistently hits the mark.

For more information, go to: www.vocalmoment.com

WHAT CAN WE LEARN FROM THE SUFFRAGETTES?

How can the exemplify Moral Courage?

The suffragette movement was a social, political, and feminist movement that existed in the late 19th and early 20th centuries. It aimed to secure women's right to vote and is most closely associated with the UK. A British newspaper initially created the term "suffragette" as a derogatory term, but the women involved in the movement embraced it.

They challenged deeply entrenched societal norms and power structures, facing ridicule, violence, and imprisonment in their quest for equality. Despite overwhelming opposition and social ostracism, it demonstrated an unwavering commitment to their cause.

Moral Courage

From 1903 to 1914, the Suffragette movement used radical protest tactics and a creative publicity campaign to advocate for women's right to vote in the UK. Their motto was **"Deeds not words,"** and over 1,000 women were imprisoned for championing this cause.

The suffragists were part of the women's suffrage movement, advocating for women's right to vote through peaceful and legal means. In 1908, they held a procession to demonstrate to Prime Minister Herbert Asquith the widespread support for women's suffrage. They lobbied parliament, marched peacefully, organised petitions, and held public meetings.

The suffragists worked tirelessly to gain support for their cause. They emphasised reasoned debate and the moral argument for equality. They believed that by demonstrating women's ability to participate in public life responsibly, they could gradually convince society and the government to extend the right to vote to women. This was instrumental in laying the groundwork for women's suffrage. **They raised awareness, educated the public, and slowly built a broad support base.**

In 1918, for the first time, over 8 million women over 30 were allowed to vote in a general election. It wasn't until 1928 that the same voting rights were applied equally to British men and women, and every man and woman over 21 was finally given the right to vote.

Betteradvocacy.org wrote **about the profound impact and legacy** of the suffragettes, including:

- *Laying the groundwork for future social justice movements.*
- *Inspiring subsequent generations to fight for equal rights for women and all minoritised groups.*
- *Setting a precedent for activism and demonstrating the power of collective action in bringing about meaningful change.*[8]

---

8 Better Advocacy https://www.betteradvocacy.org/post/from-militancy-to-pacifism-the-evolution-of-suffragette-and-suffragist-tactics

How can you Learn from their Example

We like to hire and conduct business with people we know, like, and trust. Moral courage can be your "true north", acting as a **magnet for moral compass-seeking people of integrity.**

The suffragettes' relentless pursuit of equality provided powerful lessons in persistence, strategy, and the courage to challenge deeply entrenched societal norms, systems, and the status quo.

You can follow their example, demonstrating how **you live and breathe your values.**

Here are six ways you can apply moral courage in your own life:

1. **Educate Yourself:** Stay informed about social issues, injustices and causes important to you. Regularly read from diverse sources, attend workshops, and engage in discussions to broaden your perspective.

2. **Start Small:** You don't need to lead a protest to show moral courage. Begin with small actions in your daily life. For example, you could correct someone who uses discriminatory language or support a colleague who's being mistreated.

3. **Build a Support Network:** Surround yourself with like-minded individuals who share your values. Having a support system can provide encouragement and strength when facing difficult situations. Join or create groups focused on social justice issues you care about.

4. **Practice Speaking Up:** Like any skill, practice improves moral courage. Start by voicing your opinions in low-stakes situations. As you become more comfortable, you'll find it easier to speak up in more challenging circumstances.

5. **Embrace Discomfort:** Moral courage often involves stepping out of your comfort zone. This is a natural part of growth and change. When you feel uncomfortable speaking up, remind yourself of the importance of your values and the potential impact of your actions.

6. **Learn from Setbacks:** Not every act of moral courage will lead to immediate positive change. When you face setbacks or adverse reactions, reflect on the experience. What can you learn? Use these experiences to refine your approach and build resilience.

You *can* lead and contribute to positive change in your community and beyond.

MORAL COURAGE IN ACTION

Marsha P. Johnson, a Black transgender woman, exemplified moral courage throughout her life as a **prominent figure** in the LGBTQ+ rights movement. Born in 1945, she faced discrimination on multiple fronts, including racism and transphobia, at a time when there was much less acceptance for trans people than there is today. She was a leading activist, particularly known for her role in the Stonewall Uprising in 1969.

On the night of June 28, 1969, the police raided the Stonewall Inn, a gay bar in New York City. Marsha was one of the people who resisted. This act of defiance, standing up against police brutality and discrimination, is often seen as a turning point for the modern LGBTQ+ rights movement. Marsha's brave participation in this event demonstrated incredible determination, resilience and moral courage. She risked **her safety and freedom to fight for the dignity and rights of her community.**

Marsha's activism demonstrated her unwavering commitment to her community despite constant challenges. She openly lived as herself at a time when doing so could result in violence, arrest, or institutionalisation. In 1970, she co-founded STAR (Street Transvestite Action Revolutionaries) with her friend Sylvia Rivera, providing housing and support to homeless LGBTQ+ youth in New York City. Her famous quote, "As long as my people don't have their rights across America, there's no reason for celebration," encapsulates her dedication to the fight for equality. Marsha's life teaches us that moral courage often requires us to **step out of our comfort zones and truly immerse ourselves in others' experiences.**

COURAGE

Exercise: The Ethical Challenge

OBJECTIVE: *Standing Up for Your Values*

This exercise aims to develop your moral courage by:

1. Exploring your reactions to an intense ethical challenge scenario.
2. Learning to reframe difficult moral situations into manageable tasks.
3. Applying moral courage concepts to real-life scenarios.
4. Practicing self-reflection and ethical awareness in the face of moral adversity.
5. Developing strategies to overcome fear and stand up for your values.
6. Building confidence in your ability to handle complex ethical challenges.

By the end of this exercise, you'll have practical tools to approach morally challenging situations with greater courage, a more positive mindset, and improved ethical decision-making skills.

Imaginary Scene

You live in a small town surrounded by beautiful countryside. This area is home to several endangered species, including a rare butterfly only found in this region. The local government has proposed a new motorway bypass to cut through this habitat, potentially destroying it forever. Your town needs new infrastructure to attract investment and create jobs.

The bypass promises to reduce traffic congestion and benefit the town economically. However, it comes at a significant environmental cost. Nature tourism supports some local businesses, and the bypass can be constructed further away from the town, protecting the rare butterflies. It would cost twice as much and need to be paid for by the town's residents with higher council rates. As a resident, you're faced with a moral dilemma: support your town's economic prosperity and development or stand up for environmental preservation.

Reflection Questions

1. How does this ethical dilemma make you feel? Can you identify the emotions that arise as you imagine yourself in this situation?

2. Now, consider how moral courage might help you in this scenario. How could standing up for your values, despite potential opposition, change your experience of this situation?

3. Think about a time when you've faced a moral challenge in your own life. How did moral courage help you overcome it?

Applying Moral Courage: Two Scenarios

Now that you've considered the concept of moral courage through the motorway bypass scenario let's apply it to real-life situations using the PACE framework: Purpose, Action, Confidence, and Excellence. Below are two scenarios to help you practice using moral courage to transform challenges.

Scenario 1 is an example that demonstrates how to apply the PACE framework to a common moral challenge. As you read through it, observe how each framework step addresses the challenge. This example will give you a model for applying PACE in your own life.

Scenario 2 is for you to complete. It presents a series of questions for each step of the PACE framework, allowing you to apply the concepts to a personal moral challenge. Take your time with this scenario, reflecting deeply on each question and writing down your thoughts. Remember, there are no right or wrong answers – the goal is to explore your ethical reactions, motivations, and growth potential.

By working through these scenarios, you'll gain practical experience using the PACE framework to develop moral courage. Let's begin!

COURAGE

Scenario 1: Witnessing workplace discrimination

PURPOSE: Recognise your inner drive for fairness and equality in the workplace. Let this motivation fuel your courage to address the discrimination you've witnessed.

ACTION: Take immediate steps to address the situation. Document the discriminatory behaviour you've observed. If appropriate, speak to the person experiencing discrimination, offering support. Report the issue through the proper channels, whether it's HR or a superior.

CONFIDENCE: As you take action to address the discrimination, notice how your confidence grows. Each step reinforces your ability to stand up for what's right and potentially inspires others to do the same.

EXCELLENCE: Reflect on how you handled the situation and identify areas for improvement. Perhaps you could educate yourself further on workplace rights and discrimination policies. Use this experience to continually refine your approach to addressing injustice in the workplace.

Scenario 2: Challenging a friend's inappropriate joke or comment

Answer the following questions to apply the PACE framework to your situation:

1. **PURPOSE**:

- *What moral challenge are you facing with your friend's inappropriate jokes or comments?*
- *Why is addressing this issue important to you?*
- *How might challenging this behaviour positively impact your friendship and social circle?*

2. **ACTION:**

- *What small, manageable step could you take today to address this issue with your friend?*

- *How can you approach the conversation in a firm and compassionate way?*
- *How will you hold yourself accountable for having this difficult conversation?*

3. **CONFIDENCE:**

- *After taking your first step to address the issue, how did you feel?*
- *What positive self-talk can you use to reinforce your decision to speak up?*
- *In what ways do you notice your confidence growing as you face this moral challenge?*

4. **EXCELLENCE:**

- *What long-term goal can you set for addressing inappropriate behaviour in your social circle?*
- *How can you use any adverse reactions or setbacks as learning opportunities?*
- *How might addressing this issue contribute to your personal growth and the growth of those around you?*

Remember to approach these questions with honesty and self-compassion. Your journey of developing moral courage is unique, and every step forward, no matter how small, is progress.

MORAL COURAGE AT YOUR PACE

Nelson Mandela's example shows us that moral courage can change the world. It reminds us that one person's unwavering commitment to their principles can bring about systemic change. His legacy inspires activists, generations and leaders worldwide to stand up for justice, equality, and human rights.

COURAGE

My three key learnings:

1. Moral courage involves standing up for what you believe is right, even facing opposition or potential consequences.

2. Nelson Mandela and the suffragettes who fought for their principles show what can be achieved with moral courage despite significant personal risks.

3. Moral courage can manifest in different ways by saying something to personal decisions like coming out. It is choosing authenticity and integrity over safety or conformity.

What are your three learnings?

CHAPTER FOUR

EMPATHETIC COURAGE

CHAPTER FOUR
Empathetic Courage

HOW OFTEN DO OTHERS WALK IN YOUR SHOES?

Servant leadership, a philosophy that prioritises serving over organisational success, offers numerous benefits. A servant leader focuses on the team's needs and helps them develop, perform well, and excel. The team can achieve the best results by sharing power and fostering a thriving culture, inspiring all involved.

Servant leaders are distinguished by their ability to walk in other people's shoes, embodying a profound empathy beyond mere understanding. They seek to understand the experiences, struggles, and perspectives of those they lead. They know that authentic leadership involves serving others, not just directing them. This empathetic courage allows servant leaders to make decisions that honour the humanity of their team. More importantly, they foster an environment of trust, respect, and collaboration, providing a sense of reassurance and security.

Viral Mehta wrote that servant leaders:

- *Want to serve first and lead second – strives to create a work environment in which people can truly express these deepest of inner drives.*

- *Recognise that the people doing the work generally have the best ideas about improving the processes they participate in.*

- *Spend significant time at the workplace, making direct observations and striving to create systemic improvements that add value to their employees' work.*[9]

---

[9] Viral Mehta "Servant Leadership: Helping People Come Alive" (Psychology Today July 20 2012) https://www.psychologytoday.com/us/blog/pay-it-forward/201207/servant-leadership-helping-people-come-alive

A servant leader in a significant technology project actively listens to their team, understanding that each member's input is crucial in navigating complex challenges. This empathetic courage involves deep listening. It helps the leader identify potential issues early and collaboratively develop effective solutions aligned with the team's strengths.

Being attuned to the needs and emotions of others strengthens relationships.

WHAT IS EMPATHETIC COURAGE?

Empathetic courage is understanding others, practising humility, and setting aside personal bias. It involves actively listening, walking in another person's shoes, and approaching situations with an open mind and heart. This type of courage requires the willingness to be vulnerable while protecting your mental health. It is not permitting someone to sap your positive energy, requiring you to acknowledge your limitations and genuinely connect with others' experiences and emotions.

For example, a leader who seeks to understand their team members' perspectives or an individual who steps out of their comfort zone to support a friend from a different cultural background demonstrates empathetic courage.

Empathetic courage is not just a virtue. It's a powerful force that can transform the world. This courage breaks the walls of self-centredness and prejudice, enabling individuals to form deeper connections and foster inclusivity. Whether it's the advocate standing up for minoritised communities, the mediator resolving conflicts by considering all viewpoints, or the parent guiding their child with patience and understanding, empathetic courage is at the heart of these actions. People with empathetic courage are instrumental in creating a more compassionate world. They transform knowledge into action, making **empathy a powerful tool for unity and positive change**, and **inspiring optimism and motivation for a better future.**

Empathetic Courage

Mother Theresa's Example

Mother Teresa, born Anjezë Gonxhe Bojaxhiu in 1910, is a shining example of selfless dedication. Her life's work among the poorest of the poor in Calcutta, India, demonstrated an extraordinary ability to connect with and understand those whose experiences were vastly different from her own.

Her journey began when she was 18 and left her home in North Macedonia to join a convent in Ireland. Her calling eventually led her to India, where she taught at a convent school. However, a train ride in 1946 profoundly changed her life. It set her on a path that would inspire millions.

During this journey, Mother Teresa experienced what she described as a "call within a call." She felt compelled to leave the comfort of her convent and work directly with the poorest and sickest people. This decision required immense empathetic courage. She had to step out of her familiar environment and immerse herself in a world of extreme poverty, disease, and suffering.

She lived among the people she served, facing the same hardships and challenges they did. At a time when leprosy was highly stigmatised and misunderstood, Mother Teresa reached out to those afflicted with the disease. She provided medical care and touched and embraced these individuals, showing them dignity and compassion when society had cast them aside.

She famously said, "If you judge people, you have no time to love them." This philosophy allowed her to help people whom others might have deemed unworthy. Her work attracted global attention and inspired others to join her mission. An organisation she started in 1950 continues today her legacy of empathetic service, running hospices, homes for orphaned children, clinics for people with HIV/AIDS, and other charity projects.

Mother Teresa's life teaches us that empathetic courage often requires us to step out of our comfort zones and truly immerse ourselves in the experiences of others. It's a powerful reminder of **the transformative power of empathy.**

MY JOURNEY WITH DEPRESSION AND EMPATHY
The Unwelcome Companion

Depression, an unwelcome companion, has been a part of my life for a long time. It's a journey that has tested my resilience, shaped my understanding of empathy, and ultimately led me to champion courage as a superhero. This path has been far from easy, but it has taught me invaluable lessons about the **power of empathy.**

My first suicide attempt was at the age of 14. I took an overdose of tablets used to control chronic asthma. A family member alerted a neighbour who was a nurse, and she took me to the hospital. The physical treatment – drinking an emetic to induce vomiting – was vile, tasting like a disgusting cocktail of flat lemonade, fermented egg, and cough medicine. But it was the emotional aftermath that proved to be the real challenge. The consultant caring for me in the children's ward was kinder than the psychiatrist I spoke with the next day.

Condescending conversations and 1980s Adolescent mental health

My experience with late 1980s adolescent mental health care was an eye-opener to the lack of empathy in the system. The care was lackadaisical, with sporadic compassion interspersed with condescending tones and a tendency to brush severe issues under the carpet. The first psychiatrist emphasised how guilty I must have felt. He did a great job reminding me of how I made others feel bad. He was like a headmaster interrogating a student caught smoking in the toilets, completely missing the point of my distress.

An older nurse told me, "How silly I was", and that most overdoses were toddlers accidentally confusing medication for sweets. She probably meant well, but she had no clue. I was scared. Younger nurses were kind, nonjudgmental, and appreciated my mental anguish. **Their warm smiles and taking the time to listen made me feel human.**

A few months later, there was an "opportunity for help", but the system and 'help' offered were almost laughable. My parents and I had an appointment with a psychiatrist at the Adolescent Mental Health Unit. We were taken into a room where a psychiatrist and a woman were waiting, sitting on armchairs. We sat down in similar chairs. There was a small coffee table in the middle. Tea and coffee in mugs were offered. The psychiatrist, a middle-aged white man with a crooked tie, spectacles as thick as a jam jar, put one sugar in the mug, stirred the coffee, and lifted the mug without removing the teaspoon. He spoke to me about receiving psychiatric care. At the same time, the teaspoon brushed through the hair of his left nostril, almost causing a nosebleed. We left with no confidence in the services available.

Proper mental health care would have made life much easier.

The Impact of Empathy

Over the years, I've had periodic bouts of clinical depression, typically occurring once a decade and lasting 2-3 years. Each episode has been a challenge and an opportunity to develop my empathetic courage and appreciate it in others.

In 2004, when depression returned, I was fortunate to have an outstanding GP who immediately arranged ongoing care and counselling. This time, I made the brave decision to tell my employer. The response from the HR Manager was beyond understanding – she went out of her way to ensure I was the priority, not the company. It was a stark contrast to my earlier encounters with mental health care. This experience showed me what proper support should look like.

Not all workplace environments are compassionate and supportive.

However, not all workplace experiences were as positive. I've also faced subtle yet persistent bullying that coincided with a severe bout of depression. It felt like having a form teacher who singled me out with digs and put-downs while being friendly to everyone else. It solidified my belief that a lack of empathy in the workplace can exacerbate mental health struggles.

The turning point was hitting rock bottom. **Overwhelmed by relentless bullying**, I took a small overdose of anti-sickness medication. In my darkest moment, I found the courage to call 000. The empathy from that point on helped with my recovery. The emergency services operator showed kindness and reassurance. The police officers and paramedics who arrived praised my bravery for seeking help and listened without judgment.

At the hospital, the staff's kindness continued. Unable to maintain eye contact, I looked away or at the floor when answering questions. Yet, they persisted in their gentle care. I voluntarily admitted myself to the psychiatric ward, where I spoke with psychiatrists and nursing staff. One nurse's comment about how common bullying victims were among their patients struck a chord – it was a **moment of validation and understanding** and was desperately needed.

Recovery was a long process, taking nearly a year. However, through Cognitive behavioural therapy (CBT) with my psychologist, I learned valuable strategies for managing both my depression and bullying. CBT is a form of psychotherapy that focuses on identifying and changing negative thought patterns and behaviours to improve mental health and well-being.

The "velvet glove, iron fist" approach – using a gentle, respectful manner to **de-escalate tension while maintaining firm boundaries – became a powerful tool.**

The Listening Medical Scan

Listening to patients is an excellent diagnostic device. This approach strengthens the doctor-patient relationship and leads to more accurate diagnoses and effective treatments. It ultimately fosters a more trusting and healing environment. In 2011, there was a series of hospital admissions. I had intense epigastric pain and elevated liver function tests. The discomfort in my upper abdomen felt like crocodile hatchlings feasting regularly with relentless bites telling me they were hungry. Despite numerous tests and scans, the cause of the pain remained elusive.

One consultant suggested an ERCP, a procedure that had nearly killed me before. The mere suggestion was terrifying. I did not schedule a follow-up appointment with him. I was unwilling to risk the potentially lethal procedure. Days later, back in a hospital with intense pain a different consultant sat beside me and said, "You are the talk of the hospital. We can't work out what is wrong with you! Start from the beginning and tell me your story."

The transformative power of listening for five minutes.

He listened intently, smiling and nodding as I recounted my health journey. He snapped his fingers and declared, "I know what's wrong with you! You have an incisional hernia." It was probably caused by the surgery in 2006. He said I should never undergo an ERCP again due to its dangers. Instead, he recommended a non-invasive MRI scan. The MRI scan confirmed that there were no issues with my liver. A few months later, I underwent successful surgery to repair the hernia. It demonstrated how a **doctor's empathetic courage can lead to better outcomes** and a more positive patient experience.

This experience underscored the importance of seeking second opinions and looking for an open ear and mind with every health professional.

WHAT CAN WE LEARN FROM CATS AND VETS?

How they use the Language of Empathy

Cats are empathetic. They are social creatures who bond with those giving them affection, attention, and love. Your role in providing these is crucial in reinforcing the bond between you and your cat. Cats like predictability and adherence to a routine. They're inquisitive and love exploring their surroundings, playful and yes, they purr when you pet them. When excited, they might rub against your legs. Cats can also be Jekyll & Hyde. One minute, all is cosy and fine. Seconds later, they are annoyed, reminding you they are a cat with sharp teeth and claws. After a few minutes, they play with a toy or purr again. Cats are … cats. For me, cats are ace.

With their impressive vocal range, cats could give opera singers a run for their money. Their screams, also known as caterwauls and yowls, are unmistakable and often signal that something is amiss. Whether it's pain, distress, or anxiety, a cat's continual screaming and howling is their way of saying, "It's time for a vet visit."

Veterinarians rely on empathy and careful listening to examine and treat cats effectively, especially when dealing with angry or stressed felines. Cats, known for their sensitivity and independence, can quickly become agitated in unfamiliar environments such as a vet's office. Understanding this, empathetic vets approach these situations with patience and calmness, knowing that the cat's aggression is often a response to fear or discomfort.

By listening to the cat's vocalisations, observing body language, and responding to subtle cues, vets can gauge the level of distress and adjust their approach accordingly. For example, a low, growling sound might indicate that the cat feels threatened, prompting the vet to slow down, employ softer handling techniques, or even pause to let the cat calm down.

Empathy drives vets to consider the cat's perspective, allowing them to create a less stressful experience by minimising loud noises, sudden movements, or rough handling. They might use soothing words, gentle touches, or even allow the cat to stay in its carrier for part of the exam. This approach helps calm the cat and ensures a more accurate and thorough examination, ultimately leading to better treatment outcomes.

Understanding cats is crucial for their wellness and happiness.

In March 2023, Dr. Lizzie Youens authored an article on cats.com discussing how felines communicate with humans. The main points were:

- *Despite long domestication, cats retain many wild traits and methods of feline communication have not altered much. Cats are always cats.*
- *They can communicate using body language, posture, vocalisations, scent, and touch.*
- *Paying attention to subtle changes in your cat's behaviour and signals can help you understand what they are trying to tell you about their needs and moods.*[10]

How can you Learn for their Example

With years of dedicated training, veterinarians employ exceptional empathetic courage daily. Their commitment is such that the cat would let them know even if they didn't. Vets excel at reading cats' non-verbal cues, paying close attention to body language, behavioural changes, and subtle signs of discomfort or distress. This skill allows the vet to understand the full context of a cat's experience without verbal communication.

Veterinarians know how to **create a calm, nonthreatening atmosphere** for their feline patients. They understand that a cat's emotional state significantly impacts the vet's ability to provide care. They **adjust their approach based on each cat's unique personality and needs**, being flexible in their methods to ensure the best possible care.

Applying empathy and diagnostic skills to work or business situations

Here are six actions you can learn from their approach:

1. **Enhance Non-Verbal Communication Skills:** Practice observing and interpreting body language and facial expressions in daily interactions. notice non-verbal cues and how they align with or contradict spoken words.

---

10 Dr. Lizzie Youens BSc (Hons) BVSc MRCVS "10 Ways Your Cat Is Communicating With You" (Cats.com March 28, 2023) https://cats.com/how-do-cats-communicate-with-humans

2. **Create Comfortable Environments:** Learn to cultivate spaces where others feel safe and at ease. Before a difficult conversation or meeting, consider how you can make the environment more welcoming and comfortable.

3. **Practise Patience:** Building trust takes time, especially with anxious or fearful people. In your next interaction with someone who seems hesitant or nervous, allow them time to adapt.

4. **Develop Flexibility in Approach:** Tailor your communication style or methods based on the needs of the individual you're interacting with. Identify one person who might benefit from a different communication approach. Try a new method in your next interaction with them.

5. **Use Gentle Persistence:** Learn to balance being persistent in providing care or support without being overly forceful or causing distress. When faced with resistance to your help or ideas, find gentle ways to maintain your offer of support without pushing too hard.

6. **Cultivate Calmness:** Work on maintaining a calm demeanour, especially in stressful or chaotic situations. Practice calming techniques, like deep breathing, that you can use in moments of stress or when dealing with agitated individuals.

Listening with empathy deepens trust and rapport.

EMPATHETIC COURAGE IN ACTION

How often do people listen to the real you? From April 2006 until July 2007, I spoke with my "Dalek" tracheotomy voice. It was often the topic of conversation. My "Dalek voice" **became a bridge, connecting me to others** in ways I hadn't anticipated. Instead of shying away from these discussions, I embraced them as opportunities to share my story and connect with others on a deeper level. This openness required a certain kind of courage – the courage to be vulnerable, expose my struggles, and invite others to talk. It **created a space for others to feel comfortable** sharing their stories and lived experiences.

Then one day, as I coughed, I noticed something different: my voice sounded more like my old self. Speaking through my diaphragm instead of my throat brought back my natural voice. I spent the next 10 to 15 minutes in the shower experimenting, learning to talk through my diaphragm and effectively saying "exterminate" to the Dalek voice.

This discovery was transformative. My family and friends were overjoyed when they heard me speak with my natural voice during our subsequent conversations. Colleagues who had never heard my natural voice were delighted to listen to the "real" Martin.

The experience of regaining my voice was not just a physical recovery but an emotional and psychological triumph. It symbolised overcoming a difficult period and reclaiming a significant part of my identity. But more than that, it taught me **the importance of patience, understanding, and humility.**

Exercise: the Empathy Challenge

OBJECTIVE: *Understanding Others, Understanding Yourself*

This exercise aims to develop your empathetic courage by:

1. Exploring your reactions to an intense empathy-requiring scenario.
2. Learning to reframe challenging interpersonal situations into manageable tasks.
3. Applying empathetic courage concepts to real-life scenarios.
4. Practicing self-reflection and emotional awareness in the face of others' distress.
5. Developing strategies to overcome discomfort and connect deeply with others.
6. Building confidence in your ability to handle complex emotional situations.

COURAGE

By the end of this exercise, you'll have practical tools to approach emotionally challenging situations with greater empathy, a more positive mindset, and improved interpersonal skills.

Imaginary Scene

It is your first day working in a data centre with vital technology infrastructure and a grumpy cat named Humphrey. Humphrey is known for his bellowing meows, and local hospital staff even call his scratches a "Humphrey special." Despite his temperament, Humphrey has gained immense popularity with 5 million followers on his YouTube channel. One day, Humphrey accidentally dislodges a cable while sleeping on a stack of them, causing a bank's system to crash. Just as you're about to start searching for the loose cable, a power outage occurs, leaving you and Humphrey in the dark. The CEO of your company calls you on your mobile, instructing you to find Humphrey, and hangs up with the words, "Good Luck!"

You use the mobile phone's torch to explore the data centre. You hear loud purrs from a feline deep in slumber and take tentative steps, finding him at the back of a large server. You know coaxing Humphrey off the cables will probably spark his explosive temper. You follow Humphrey on YouTube and know how angry he gets! You don't want a Humphrey scar on your hands and arms. You kneel and extend your arms with your hands touching Humphrey's back. You hear a Meow louder than a jumbo jet taking off. Expecting a painful bite and sharp claws, you notice a tongue-licking of your fingers. Seconds later, Humphrey leaps into your arms and purrs. He likes you! You record a video and upload it on YouTube. You are the first person ever to hold Humphrey!

Reflection Questions

1. How does this challenging scenario with Humphrey make you feel? Can you identify the emotions that arise as you imagine yourself in this situation?

2. Consider how empathetic courage might help you in this scenario. How could understanding and connecting with Humphrey, despite your fear, change your experience of this situation?

3. Think about a time when you've faced a challenging interpersonal situation in your own life. How did empathetic courage help you overcome it?

Now that you've considered the concept of empathetic courage through the Humphrey scenario let's apply it to real-life situations using the PACE framework: Purpose, Action, Confidence, and Excellence.

Below are two scenarios to help you practice using empathetic courage to transform challenges.

Scenario 1 is an example that demonstrates how to apply the PACE framework to a common empathy-requiring challenge. As you read through it, observe how each step of the framework addresses the challenge. This example will give you a model for applying PACE in your own life.

Scenario 2 is for you to complete. It presents a series of questions for each step of the PACE framework, allowing you to apply the concepts to a personal challenge requiring empathy. Take your time with this scenario, reflecting deeply on each question and writing down your thoughts. Remember, there are no right or wrong answers – the goal is to explore your emotional reactions, motivations, and potential for growth.

By working through these scenarios, you'll gain practical experience using the PACE framework to develop empathetic courage. Let's begin!

Scenario 1: Calming an upset colleague during a high-stress project

PURPOSE: Recognise your inner drive to create a supportive work environment and maintain team harmony. Let this motivation fuel your courage to approach and understand your distressed colleague.

COURAGE

ACTION: Take immediate steps to address the situation. Find a quiet, private space to talk with your colleague. Approach them calmly and without judgment, like carefully moving towards Humphrey. Listen actively to their concerns without interrupting, as you would listen for the cat's location.

CONFIDENCE: As you engage in this empathetic conversation, notice how your confidence grows. Each step in understanding and supporting your colleague reinforces your ability to navigate difficult interpersonal situations.

EXCELLENCE: Reflect on how you handled the situation and identify areas for improvement. Perhaps you could learn more about stress management techniques to share with your team. Use this experience to refine your approach to continually supporting colleagues during high-stress periods.

Scenario 2: Helping a friend through a personal crisis

Answer the following questions to apply the PACE framework to your situation:

PURPOSE:

- *What specific empathy challenge are you facing with your friend's crisis?*
- *Why is offering empathetic support important to you in this situation?*
- *What broader personal values are you upholding by offering empathy and support?*

ACTION:

- *What small, manageable step could you take today to begin supporting your friend empathetically?*
- *How can you create a calm, safe space for your friend to open up, similar to your careful approach with Humphrey?*

- How will you balance being supportive with maintaining healthy personal boundaries?

CONFIDENCE:

- After taking your first step to support your friend, how did you feel?
- What positive self-talk can you use to reinforce your ability to offer empathy and support?
- In what ways do you notice your confidence growing as you navigate this emotionally challenging situation?

EXCELLENCE:

- What long-term goal can you set for developing your empathetic skills?
- How can you use moments of discomfort or uncertainty as learning opportunities?
- How might developing your empathetic courage contribute to your personal growth and the quality of your relationships?

Remember to approach these questions with honesty and self-compassion. Your journey of developing empathetic courage is unique, and every step forward, no matter how small, is progress.

WRAP UP

Dealing with emotional situations requires patience, understanding, and the courage to stay present even when things are uncomfortable. Veterinarians do this every day with an assortment of ferocious felines. Empathetic courage enables you to navigate challenging interpersonal situations more effectively, successfully and compassionately.

Be patient with yourself as you grow and celebrate the moments when you successfully **connect with others on a deeper level.** Your efforts in

COURAGE

developing empathetic courage will benefit those around you and enrich your life experiences.

My three key learnings:

1. Empathetic courage involves stepping out of our comfort zones to truly understand and connect with others, even when their experiences differ significantly from ours.

2. Veterinarians are confident in giving cats lousy news.

3. Developing empathetic courage requires consistent practice and self-reflection. It involves balancing genuine care for others with maintaining healthy personal boundaries.

What are Your three learnings?

CHAPTER FIVE

STEADFAST COURAGE

CHAPTER FIVE
Steadfast Courage

HOW DO YOU LEARN FROM FAILURES AND MISTAKES?

All your failed exams and mistakes helped shape you into who you are now. Continuing to learn from them and adapting is a recipe for achieving. It is a crucial component of growth, replacing a spoke in the wheel with a sprocket, peddling you forward to delivering outcomes and sustainable success. Quitting is easy, and passing the first time is commendable.

Failing and then passing provides the gift of wisdom and the knowledge to access insight – highlighting what did not work and areas for improvement.

When viewed through the lens of growth, every failure and mistake become stepping stones toward eventual achievement. Instead of being seen as setbacks, failures should be embraced as opportunities to refine strategies, enhance skills, and build resilience. They teach you how to use steadfast courage and guide you into better decision-making.

Radu Atanasiu Ph.D advised the major points of learning from failure are:

- Failure illuminates what we need to unlearn, what we need to learn instead, and what we need to do about it.

- This triple insight can be articulated into simple rules that sound like proverbs.

- Learning from failure is more powerful and lasts longer.[11]

---

[11] "What Exactly Do We Learn from Failure?" (Psychology Today September 28, 2023) https://www.psychologytoday.com/us/blog/to-choose-or-not-to-choose/202309/what-exactly-do-we-learn-from-failure

COURAGE

The process of learning from mistakes begins with accepting and acknowledging them. This involves setting aside ego and defensiveness to assess what went wrong honestly. By taking ownership of failures, you can analyse the causes and prepare better for the next time. This reflection allows for identifying knowledge gaps that can prevent similar mistakes in the future.

Steadfast courage is your orchestra rehearsing with you for your magnificence.

WHAT IS STEADFAST COURAGE?

Steadfast courage is being resolute, focused, and purposeful. It involves maintaining determination and commitment to a goal, regardless of obstacles or setbacks. It's not giving up, even when the path forward is difficult. It transforms something that is not quite right into something better. For instance, an entrepreneur persevering through multiple business failures or an athlete continuing to train despite numerous injuries. Breaking the status quo requires steadfast courage. Great innovators like Thomas Edison evoked this type of courage. He famously conducted thousands of unsuccessful experiments before inventing the light bulb.

It was a relentless pursuit of innovation and improvement.

Steadfast courage is the catalyst that shatters the walls of doubt and adversity. It empowers you to remain true to your mission. It is the scientist who persists in research despite years of inconclusive results. The activist who tirelessly advocates for change. The student diligently pursuing their education. By staying focused and purposeful, people with steadfast courage achieve their goals and inspire others with perseverance. It transforms determination into success. It turns persistence into a potent force for personal and collective achievement. **This unyielding focus and dedication are the hallmarks of great innovators, and anyone committed to making a meaningful impact.**

Women Boxers' Example

In ancient times, women did not compete in boxing or most other sports. Women boxers were often a novelty act during the modern era, participating in contests held in London during the 1700s. Women's boxing was featured in the 1904 Olympics, but only as a display event.

For 108 years, women were excluded from Olympic boxing due to traditional gender roles and **misconceptions about the sport's suitability for women.** This exclusion persisted despite women's participation in other combat sports and their longstanding involvement in amateur and professional boxing.

It wasn't until the 2012 London Olympics that female boxers were finally allowed to compete, marking a pivotal moment in the sport's history. This historic inclusion came after years of **relentless advocacy by trailblazing women** who refused to be sidelined. At these Games, 36 women from different countries competed across three weight classes, while men competed in ten weight classes. In the Tokyo 2020 Olympics, the women's weight classes increased to five and the men's reduced to eight. At The Paris 2024 Olympics, 248 boxers could participate equally between men and women. The male boxers contested matches in seven weight classes and the women in six.

The road to women competing in Olympic boxing was paved with numerous Mt. Everest-sized challenges. Many countries, including Australia, had official bans on women's boxing until the early 2000s. These bans highlighted the extent of systemic exclusion in boxing and the time it takes for positive change to occur. Women continued to train, compete in non-Olympic events, and advocate for their right to participate at the highest level of their sport. **Their unwavering commitment eventually led to change.**

Out LGBTQ+ women boxers became Olympic Champions, and several became professional world champions. They have been particularly influential. Their success and openness about their sexuality have made them inspiring figures, breaking barriers in boxing and other combat sports. Their trailblazing has **opened doors for future generations** with their success and visibility, challenging outdated norms and inspiring many. These women are helping to grow the acceptance of LGBTQ+ athletes in boxing.

Muhammad Ali said,

"He who is not courageous enough to take risks will accomplish nothing in life."

The courageous women boxers took risks, which led to outstanding accomplishments.

THE STEADFAST STARK STORY

The real story is Better than Fiction

I'm a Stark who has never watched Game of Thrones or Iron Man. Fictional stories pale in comparison to the real thing: our stories of real-life challenges and triumphs.

What I have faced and overcome are relatable anecdotes of authentic juggernaut struggles and jubilant exultations. The Stark Clan and my cousin Tony are steadfast in their support. Courageous true-life tales are more intriguing than superhero movies or fantasy soap operas.

A source of inspiration could be your friends, family or your story.

Successfully managing Addison's disease requires developing a knack for knowing the story chapter and verse. **It is my survival guide. This is a life-saving skill.** Early intervention stops an adrenal crisis from worsening and enables rapid recovery. It's like someone with arachnophobia realising the spider lurks under the pillow. Someone needs to remove it before the situation escalates.

The Brush with Death that changed everything

In late 2017, I experienced an Addisonian crisis that almost killed me—the day started fine and dandy. Feeling under the weather, I took a precautionary dose of hydrocortisone before heading to work to tackle the emails and tasks. A general malaise persisted throughout the morning, but I shrugged it off as a cold manifesting. The priority was advising a stakeholder on solving a critical business issue. I started writing an email, but it was not sent. My condition worsened. The malaise intensified, and I started feeling dizzy and developed lower abdominal pain – classic signs of an Addisonian crisis. Still underestimating the severity, I took another dose of hydrocortisone and decided to head home. The situation quickly worsened.

Upon reaching my apartment, the simple act of walking upstairs sapped all my energy. I collapsed on the floor after opening the door. **Urgent action was required.** I administered an intramuscular cortisone injection into my thigh. This rapidly provided the cortisol my body desperately needed. Injecting cortisone into a large muscle enables it to be quickly absorbed into the bloodstream. The 000 operator understood the criticality of my situation.

Every step of the healthcare system worked in perfect harmony, saving my life.

A paramedic arrived within five minutes. My blood pressure was dangerously low, my pulse shallow and slow, and nausea overtook me. The paramedic swiftly inserted a cannula and attached a bag of fluids, vital steps in stabilising my condition. Two more paramedics arrived shortly after, and I was rushed to the hospital. Upon arrival, I was triaged as a Category 1 patient – the most critical classification, requiring immediate attention and promptly taken to the resuscitation (Resus) section of the emergency department.

As I was wheeled into Resus, painful memories of previous ICU stays flooded back. The larger monitoring screens, the more powerful blood pressure machine, the brighter lights – everything was amplified, mirroring the gravity of my condition. Attached to an array of machinery, I watched as the screen displayed my pulse and blood pressure, both alarmingly low. Dizziness, worsening nausea, and fear gripped me. Panic would achieve nothing.

I summoned my courage, reminding myself I was in the best possible hands.

The medical staff worked with unflappable efficiency, rushing fluids through my body and administering a high dosage of hydrocortisone intravenously. If this didn't work, my only chance of survival might be to be placed on a ventilator – a prospect that filled me with dread. It was a surreal experience, like sitting on a flight deck behind pilots expertly navigating extreme turbulence. The medical staff exuded a soothing confidence that understood the gravity of the situation, communicating exactly what they needed to do and just getting on with it.

Within an hour, I was out of danger. Later, when admitted to a ward, I reflected on the day's events. Something about this experience was tinged with déjà vu. The memories of the ICU contaminated my perception of reality, trapping me in a vicious loop of false memories. The pain of the previous trauma was like a genie refusing to return to its bottle. My mind connected the dots between this experience and my painful, traumatic time in the ICU years before. It created a deep bond with the relatable experience and formed PTSD.

This brush with death taught me the true meaning of steadfast courage. It wasn't about grand gestures or heroic acts but the daily commitment to managing my health. The willingness to act swiftly in moments of crisis. **The determination to keep living and thriving despite the challenges posed by my condition.**

The Sport waiting for Martin

My emotional healing involved speaking with a counsellor, the support of family and close friends, and something radical. I never expected the radical thing to be boxing! Taking a private self-defence class introduced me to basic boxing moves. Putting on boxing gloves for the first time felt like an invitation to join a community I didn't know I needed.

Before long, I was hitting pads and bags, learning foot drills, and mastering the art of the jab, cross, hook, rip, and uppercut. The sound of a perfectly landed punch on the pads became my new anthem of resilience. It had the roar of a rocket launching into space, symbolising my ascent from the depths of my health struggles. Boxing became more than just a sport; **it was a form of therapy. It allowed me to own and break through my painful memories with each punch.**

WHAT CAN WE LEARN FROM THE BYGONE ERA
How they Survived Steadfast Courage

During the Edwardian era in the UK, one and a half million British people lived and worked as servants in grand houses. Classic British costume dramas such as Upstairs Downstairs and Downton Abbey provide a glimpse of what their lives would have been like. Gruelling conditions and long hours were the norm. Yet, they overwhelmingly maintained an unwavering commitment to delivering an impeccable service.

In the morning, the servants started their work by tending to the family's needs before caring for their own. Housemaids would quietly go up the back stairs, carrying fresh water and covered slop pails to avoid being seen or heard. They would empty chamber pots, clear cold ashes from the fireplace, bring up coal, light a new fire, and clean up any messes from the day before without disturbing their masters.

The servants often worked 16-hour days. They maintained a constant state of readiness and anticipated needs. The physical demands were immense, from carrying heavy trays up multiple flights of stairs to polishing vast amounts of silver and brass. They were expected always to remain invisible, silent, and emotionally composed. They had to suppress their needs and emotions to cater to their employers' whims, which required immense self-control and perseverance.

COURAGE

The rigid hierarchy within the servant class itself added another layer of complexity. Each servant had to know their place and perform their specific duties flawlessly. Perhaps most remarkably, many servants maintained a sense of pride in their work and loyalty to the houses they served despite the thankless nature of their jobs.

This steadfast dedication, often lasting decades or even entire lifetimes is a testament to their courage and resilience.

It is not enough to survive in the work environment; employees must thrive.

In October 2021, the Harvard Business Review published the following strategies to improve employee health and well-being:

1. Give workers more control over how they do their work.
2. Allow employees more flexibility about when and where they work.
3. Increase the stability of workers' schedules.
4. Provide employees with opportunities to identify and solve workplace problems.
5. Keep your organisation adequately staffed so workloads are reasonable.
6. Encourage managers in your organisation to support employees' personal needs.
7. Take steps to foster a sense of social belonging among employees.[12]

How can you Heal from their Example

You probably don't need to carry heavy buckets of hot water upstairs just for someone else to have a hot bath while all you have access to is a small

---

[12] Erin L. Kelly, Lisa F. Berkman, Laura D. Kubzansky, and Meg Lovejoy "7 Strategies to Improve Your Employees' Health and Well-Being" (Harvard Business Review October 12, 2021) https://hbr.org/2021/10/7-strategies-to-improve-your-employees-health-and-well-being

sink with a cold tap. The servants of the Edwardian era found pride in their work despite the intense conditions and considerable difficulties.

Purpose and perseverance can help you find meaning in your work. Developing steadfast courage enables you to persist with obstacles and roadblocks. Here are six practical, steadfast steps you can apply from the Edwardian era servants:

1. **Maintainable and Achievable Standards:** Servants were expected to deliver perfection consistently. Set standards you can achieve, strive to meet them, learn from failure, and adapt.

2. **Develop Emotional Resilience:** Servants had to maintain composure in the face of criticism and unfair treatment. Practice emotional control under challenging situations, pause, take a deep breath and respond calmly.

3. **Anticipate Needs:** Good servants predicted their employers' needs before being asked. In your work or relationships, try to anticipate others' needs and address them proactively.

4. **Persistence in Repetitive Tasks:** Much of a servant's work was repetitive and mundane. Find meaning and purpose in your routines. Choose a repetitive task you don't enjoy and find ways to do it.

5. **Adaptability:** Servants had to adapt to changing situations and expectations. Cultivate flexibility and the ability to adjust without losing focus. Intentionally change one of your routines. Notice your reaction and practice adapting quickly and positively to this change.

6. **Maintain Dignity in All Circumstances:** Despite their low social status, many servants maintained a sense of dignity and pride in their work. Preserve your self-respect and professionalism, regardless of your position or how others treat you.

Purposefully focusing on what matters builds a firm resolve.

STEADFAST COURAGE IN ACTION

Steadfast courage can be found in families' **hearts, minds, and memories**. Think of your favourite homemade treat and the person who created it. No one else can make it as good as they can. My nan was a pastry cook in the 1920s. She worked in a large house, conjuring wondrous and magical meals. I know because of the delicious treats she baked for her grandchildren.

Nan **harnessed the skills** she learnt from her time in service. She included them in her cooking repertoire, making the world's best apple and blackberry pie. There was something about the way she made pastry. People often say that a fine dessert melts in your mouth. One bite of Nan's pie, and you can instantly feel the crumbling pastry. It gives you a dopamine hit of love and support.

The pastry's texture, baked apple, and blackberry fusion were a local legend. Everyone we spoke to knew about Nan's pie and **how it made them feel.** She spent hours in the kitchen during the week making her magical creations for family visits on a Saturday afternoon. I experienced Nan's love in every bite.

Exercise: The Persistence Challenge

OBJECTIVE: *Persevering Through Challenges*

This exercise aims to develop your steadfast courage by:

1. Exploring your reactions to a challenging, persistence-requiring scenario.
2. Learning to reframe complex long-term tasks into manageable steps.
3. Applying steadfast courage concepts to real-life scenarios.
4. Practicing self-reflection and resilience in the face of ongoing challenges.

5. Developing strategies to overcome setbacks and maintain a commitment to your goals.

6. Building confidence in your ability to persevere through complex, long-term tasks.

By the end of this exercise, you'll have practical tools to approach challenging situations with more remarkable persistence, a more positive mindset, and improved problem-solving skills for long-term goals.

Imaginary Scene

Bake my Nan's apple and blackberry pie!

It's impossible!

(While this scene is brief, it encapsulates the challenge of recreating a cherished family recipe that seems unattainable, requiring patience, attention to detail, and perseverance – key elements of steadfast courage.)

Reflection Questions

1. How does the challenge of recreating this seemingly impossible recipe make you feel? Can you identify the emotions that arise as you imagine yourself attempting this task?

2. Consider how steadfast courage might help you in this scenario. How could maintaining determination and commitment, despite initial failures, change your experience of this challenge?

3. Think about a time when you've faced a long-term challenge in your own life that seemed impossible at first. How did steadfast courage help you overcome it?

Now that you've considered the concept of steadfast courage through the apple and blackberry pie scenario let's apply it to real-life situations using the PACE framework: Purpose, Action, Confidence, and Excellence.

COURAGE

Below are two scenarios to help you practice using steadfast courage to transform challenges.

Scenario 1 is an example that demonstrates how to apply the PACE framework to a common challenge requiring persistence. As you read through it, observe how each step of the framework addresses the challenge. This example will give you a model for applying PACE in your own life.

Scenario 2 is for you to complete. It presents a series of questions for each step of the PACE framework, allowing you to apply the concepts to a personal challenge requiring steadfast courage. Take your time with this scenario, reflecting deeply on each question and writing down your thoughts. Remember, there are no right or wrong answers – the goal is to explore your reactions, motivations, and potential for growth in the face of long-term challenges.

By working through these scenarios, you'll gain practical experience in using the PACE framework to develop steadfast courage. Let's begin!

Scenario 1: Learning a new skill for career advancement

PURPOSE: Recognise your inner drive for professional growth and the long-term benefits of acquiring this new skill. Let this motivation fuel your courage to persist through the learning process.

ACTION: Take immediate steps to begin your learning journey. Research learning resources, set a structured study schedule and start with the fundamentals of the new skill. Break down the learning process into smaller, manageable tasks, like breaking down the steps of baking a complex pie.

CONFIDENCE: As you progress in learning the new skill, notice how your confidence grows. Each small achievement reinforces your ability to master complex tasks and adapt to new challenges in your career.

EXCELLENCE: Reflect on your learning process and identify areas for improvement. Perhaps you could find more efficient study methods or seek additional practice opportunities. Use this experience to refine your approach to learning and professional development continually.

Scenario 2: Advocating for a cause in your community

Answer the following questions to apply the PACE framework to your situation:

PURPOSE:

- What specific long-term challenge are you facing in advocating for your cause?
- Why is this cause important to you, and how does it align with your values?
- What broader societal changes are you working towards through this advocacy?

ACTION:

- What small, manageable step could you take today to begin your advocacy journey?
- How can you break down your long-term advocacy goals into smaller, achievable milestones?
- How will you maintain your commitment when faced with setbacks or slow progress?

CONFIDENCE:

- After taking your first steps in advocacy, how did you feel?
- What positive self-talk can you use to reinforce your ability to create change?
- In what ways do you notice your confidence growing as you persist in your advocacy efforts?

EXCELLENCE:

- What long-term goal can you set for your advocacy efforts?
- How can you use setbacks or challenges as learning opportunities to improve your approach?
- How might your persistent efforts in this cause contribute to your personal growth and leadership skills?

Remember to approach these questions with honesty and self-reflection. Your journey of developing steadfast courage is unique, and every step forward, no matter how small, contributes to your long-term success and impact.

WRAP UP

Achieving any significant objective requires patience, practice, and perseverance. It demands steadfast courage. You can overcome obstacles with steadfast courage by breaking down big challenges into smaller steps and consistently working towards your goal. It transforms what **might initially seem impossible into a reality.**

Adopting steadfast courage is a wise investment of your time. Most "overnight successes" did not just do something yesterday. They spent years working **hard and smart, building a solid foundation as a launchpad for sustainable achievements.**

My three key learnings:

1. Steadfast courage is unwavering resolve in facing challenges. It transforms difficulties into opportunities for growth and innovation.
2. My brush with death taught me the true meaning of being resolute, focused, purposeful, and finding meaning after a crisis.
3. Steadfast courage can be passed down through generations. My Nan's apple and blackberry pie symbolises love, skill, and perseverance.

Steadfast Courage

What are your three learnings

CHAPTER SIX

CEREBRAL COURAGE

CHAPTER SIX
Cerebral Courage

HOW DO YOU TURN YOUR IDEAS INTO ACCOMPLISHMENTS?

Successful innovators possess a remarkable talent for creative thinking. They envision endless possibilities, overcoming obstacles with a growth mindset that turns barriers into opportunities. Their journey begins with a clear vision – an idea to solve a problem or meet a need, whether by improving existing products or creating novel solutions. Achievement comes through meticulous planning, adaptability and persistence. They use foresight and communicate their vision confidently.

History abounds with world-changing individuals. Take Alan Turing, famous for breaking the Enigma code during World War II. His persistence and unconventional thinking enabled him to transform complex ideas into practical solutions. Turing's work illustrates how a well-executed idea can have profound, lasting impacts. His contributions are believed to have shortened the war by years, saving millions of lives.

In July 2021, Eric Haseltine Ph.D. published an article about the psychology of innovation highlighting:

- *Innovations require people to change behaviours, so an ability to motivate behaviour change and traits such as creativity is needed.*

- *Nurturing informal relationships founded on trust encourages people in those relationships to risk adopting radical new ways of doing things.*

- *A good way for innovators to make game-changing ideas succeed is to foster loose, informal social networks.*[13]

---

[13] Eric Haseltine Ph.D. "The Surprising Psychology of Innovation: (Psychology Today July 27, 2021) https://www.psychologytoday.com/us/blog/long-fuse-big-bang/202107/the-surprising-psychology-innovation

One crucial aspect of turning ideas into reality is embracing collaboration. Many successful innovations result from teamwork, where diverse perspectives and skills combine to refine and improve an initial idea. Innovators like Turing understood the value of drawing on the strengths of others, working with a team of cryptanalysts to achieve what seemed impossible.

Turning ideas into accomplishments is about the journey from inspiration to realisation.

WHAT IS CEREBRAL COURAGE?

Cerebral courage is disruption, innovation, and driving change. It involves challenging established norms, thinking critically, and pursuing transformative new ideas. It temporarily worries the worrisome and troubles the troublesome until they see your magic and want you to cast a spell for them. It is about intellectual bravery and a willingness to explore uncharted territories. You question conventional wisdom. You think creatively about finding solutions others overlook and wish they had discovered.

Cerebral courage breaks through the walls of complacency and tradition. It is the courage of the mind. It empowers individuals to pioneer new pathways.

The entrepreneur who disrupts an entire industry with a novel business model, the scientist who proposes a revolutionary theory, or the educator who implements innovative teaching methods to enhance learning. This courage is the engine behind the relentless pursuit of a better future.

It is not just a concept. It's a call to action and a beacon of hope for those who dare to dream and strive for a better future.

Helen Keller's Example

Helen Keller, born in 1880, is an extraordinary example of mental fortitude. At 19 months old, she was afflicted by an illness that rendered her deaf and blind. Despite this, she used her unyielding spirit and intellectual courage to turn her challenges into a catalyst for significant change and inspiration.

Her first breakthrough came when Anne Sullivan became her teacher, introducing her to language through touch. This sparked a revolution in Keller's mind, demonstrating her remarkable ability to think creatively and find solutions others had overlooked. She learned to read Braille, use sign language, and talk.

Keller was a prolific author who wrote 14 books and numerous articles. Despite never having heard or seen language used, she expressed complex ideas and emotions. She advocated for people with disabilities, women's suffrage, and other social causes. Her advocacy work showcased her ability to envision and work towards a more inclusive future. Keller travelled worldwide, giving lectures and challenging societal perceptions about disability. She used her unique perspective to illuminate social inequalities.

She didn't just adapt to her circumstances; she revolutionised perceptions of what was possible. Her innovative approaches to communication and learning paved the way for new educational methods for people with disabilities. Helen Keller's life is a testament to the transformative power of cerebral courage. She pushed the boundaries of what was possible, challenged conventional wisdom, and accelerated progress.

HISTORY INSPIRES A BETTER FUTURE

The Gay World Boxing Megastar

History teaches us what's possible. In 2021, I was interviewed for a TV documentary series about the history of LGBTQ+ people in sports. My segment focused on homophobia in boxing and highlighted the story of a trailblazer who faced racism and homophobia to become a world champion. My purpose involves correcting past wrongs and removing

COURAGE

discrimination and barriers. Alfonso Teofilo Brown, known as Panama Al Brown, was born in 1902, the same year as my granddad. Brown was the first Latin American to win a world boxing championship.

When contemplating a better future, we can look to the past for trailblazers who disrupted, innovated, and changed things.

Brown's exceptional journey began in Panama, where his natural boxing talent was apparent. He stood at 5 foot 11, an impressive height for a bantamweight. His reach and agility struck fear into his opponents. As a Black gay man in the early 20th century, he faced widespread racism in both Latin America and the United States, where he built his career. **However, his skill in the ring could not be denied.** In 1920s New York, he gained recognition for his exceptional boxing abilities.

Brown's boxing style balanced speed, technical skill, and strategic intelligence with graceful movement and precise punches. He was known as "The Ballet Dancer of the Ring." His natural talent and dedication to training led him to become the World Bantamweight Champion in 1929, a title he held until 1935. He was open about his identity as a gay man. Despite scrutiny and discrimination, **he remained unapologetically himself.** While pursuing his successful boxing career in Paris, he led a parallel life as a performance artist. He became a prominent figure in the vibrant nightlife scene and worked alongside Josephine Baker, challenging the racism of the time with their performances.

What would Life be like for him today?

I imagine what he could have achieved today. Panama Al Brown might have headlined events at Madison Square Garden as a world champion boxer and renowned artist, sharing the stage with global icons like Rihanna and Beyoncé. I see him integrating his boxing fame with his love for music and performance, amassing millions of social media followers and entertaining crowds of millions worldwide. His legacy embodies resilience, talent, and a spirit that transcended the oppressive social norms of his time.

His life of honesty, transparency and generosity continues to inspire and educate us today.

My new passion

In May 2018, I experienced another severe Addisonian crisis and was admitted to Resus. This compounded my PTSD, making self-care a bigger priority. My mind said, "Martin, you are strong enough to face anything!" It was like allowing a boxer to punch me without punching him back. A referee quickly stops the fight when a boxer is not punching their opponent. I learnt a life lesson through shadowboxing. It is a training exercise in which a boxer practices throwing punches, defensive movements, and footwork in the air without an opponent. It was a mental representation of my health challenge.

I grasped that overcoming the discomfort of punching my imaginary opponent was my spirit shouting, "You matter!"

Boxing gave me a new sense of freedom in life – the kind that allows you to dream big without any barnacles. It's akin to the feeling of booking a holiday before the era of social media and influencers. Discussing past holiday experiences with friends would prompt you to visit a travel agent, pick up brochures, and see yourself jetting off to an exciting part of the world.

Practising the drills and combinations from class improved my footwork, and my confidence flourished. The gym had a small collection of boxing gloves that smelled like a small mountain of old sneakers worn by cross-country runners. I purchased a pair of boxing gloves. It was an investment in me! Other boxers training at the gym shared tips and encouraged me. **I was now part of the boxing family.**

A leadership opportunity.

I catalogued my journey on Instagram using the hashtag #gayboxing, noticing fewer than 1,000 posts. The hashtag #boxing had more than 20 million! People used to joke, "Martin can't punch his way out of a paper bag!" After a few months, friends asked how my boxing training was going.

Boxing helped with the PTSD recovery. It wasn't a security blanket but a springboard for new opportunities and a path in life. A pathway of leading global change and tackling one of the most stubborn problems in sport to solve – homophobia!

History-making was my future.

WHAT CAN WE LEARN FROM STEVE JOBS?

How he Innovated with Cerebral Courage

Steve Jobs famously said, "People don't know what they want until you show it to them." This statement encapsulates his innovative thinking and willingness to challenge conventional wisdom. Jobs envisioned a functional, elegant, and user-friendly machine when clunky and expensive personal computers were the norm.

He disrupted the technology industry by **overlooking restrictions that others took for granted.** His bold vision led to the creation of Apple and the revolutionary Macintosh. Jobs' embodiment of cerebral courage was probably most apparent in his approach to product development. His famous "reality distortion field" was a testament to his ability to inspire others to think beyond perceived limitations. He **ignored doubt and skepticism** from peers and industry leaders to pursue his vision.

Steve Jobs' cerebral courage extended beyond his product innovations to his leadership style and philosophy. He believed in the power of focus and was unafraid to make difficult decisions to streamline Apple's product line. He famously reduced the company's offerings to just a few core products. This focus allowed Apple to **concentrate on excellence and a better fit for customers.** It led to breakthroughs that others in the industry couldn't match.

He courageously led Apple through intense innovation, developing iconic products such as the iPod, iPhone, and iPad. These devices improved existing technologies and **fundamentally changed how people interacted with the world.**

Forbes published an article about Steve Jobs' legacy highlighting:

- *He had an uncanny sense of what a consumer might want in the way of technology, driving Apple's innovation in this direction.*

- *His philosophy was based on his belief that the computing experience should be easy to use and intuitive.*

- *Starting in the early 2000s, not long after his cancer diagnosis, was to begin the serious process of grooming his successor.*[14]

How can you Learn from his Example

Steve Jobs' legacy as a disruptor and innovator is **inseparable from his cerebral courage.** He consistently pushed the boundaries of what was possible, challenged conventional thinking, and turned bold ideas into world-changing realities.

Are you willing to take considered risks? What would you like to change in your industry **or** profession? Disruptive and creative thinking can leave **an indelible mark on your business and customers**. It can improve the product and service experience.

Here are six ways you can learn from Steve Jobs:

1. **Persistence in the face of adversity:** Jobs' determination to continue working and innovating despite his illness is a powerful example of courage. When facing your challenges, remember that persistence can lead to remarkable achievements.

---

[14] Tim Bajarin Contributor "Steve Jobs' Legacy Still Drives Apple's Current And Future Products" (Forbes Oct 7, 2019 https://www.forbes.com/sites/timbajarin/2019/10/07/steve-jobs-legacy-still-drives-apples-current-and-future-products/

2. **Embracing discomfort for growth:** Jobs was known for pushing himself and others out of their comfort zones. This willingness to embrace discomfort often led to groundbreaking innovations.

3. **Maintaining focus on long-term goals:** Despite physical setbacks, Jobs never lost sight of his vision for Apple. This teaches us the importance of keeping our eyes on our ultimate goals, even when facing immediate physical challenges.

4. **Taking care of your health**: While Jobs' work ethic was admirable, it's also essential to learn from his eventual recognition of the need to prioritise health. Balance your drive with self-care.

5. **Using limitations as motivation:** Jobs turned his health challenges into motivation to achieve more in the time he had. Consider how you can use your limitations as fuel for your ambitions.

6. **Cultivating resilience:** Jobs' ability to bounce back from setbacks, both in his health and business, exemplifies the importance of resilience in cerebral courage.

You *can* think differently and make a positive impact.

CEREBRAL COURAGE IN ACTION

The 2019 Sydney Gay and Lesbian Mardi Gras parade became a pivotal moment in my journey of cerebral courage. Here, I transformed a personal statement into a powerful visual metaphor for bravery and identity. The word "courage" was painted on my back in bold letters. This was **a nod to the past and a powerful look to the future.**

While most of my heritage is English, I have Scottish blood from both sides of the family. The percentage is immaterial to me. Stark is a sept of the Robertson Clan. A sept is a division of a clan. I have a strong affinity for this part of my ancestry, **rooted in a welcoming, vibrant community and a sense of belonging.** I chose to wear the Stark family tartan, marching with the Scottish group Bravehearts.

Shortly before the parade, a photograph was taken. I call it Kilted Courage. I was looking forward. My blue-dyed hair enhanced the traditional tartan with the word "courage" prominently displayed. This image captured more than just a moment; it encapsulated a journey of cerebral courage, daring to be visible and **proudly owning every aspect of my identity.** Two years later, the photograph would be the lead image in a CNN article about me disrupting homophobia in boxing.

This experience taught me the true power of cerebral courage. It's not just about internal resolve; it's about finding innovative ways to express oneself and advocate for change. The "kilted courage" concept emerged from this experience – **a unique blend of tradition and progress**, honouring one's roots while **boldly stepping into a more inclusive future.**

Exercise: Innovative Pitching

OBJECTIVE: *Embracing Disruption and Fostering Innovation*

This exercise aims to develop your cerebral courage by:

1. Exploring your reactions to an innovative business pitch scenario.
2. Learning to reframe unconventional ideas into compelling opportunities.
3. Applying cerebral courage concepts to real-life scenarios.
4. Practicing creative thinking and resilience in the face of skepticism.
5. Develop strategies to overcome the fear of rejection and stand by innovative ideas.
6. Building confidence in your ability to present and defend unconventional concepts.

By the end of this exercise, you'll have practical tools to approach innovative challenges with greater cerebral courage, a more creative mindset, and improved problem-solving skills.

COURAGE

Imaginary Scene

You are an entrepreneur pitching biodegradable glitter on Shark Tank. The glitter is made from vegetable peelings, which you can only see for one day. Traditional glitter is made of non-porous materials like aluminium, and the shiny particles adhere to surfaces when they dry. Most biodegradable glitters don't have the same sparkle, but your product does. You only have two prototypes and shared the first one on social media. The producer of Shark Tank saw the post and invited you to the studio the next day. You had no time to prepare and take the prototype with you.

It is the final show of Season 20. In the green room, you hear Frank, the billionaire Shark who has never invested, say, "I have had enough of all the silly sparkly products!" Someone nudges your arm, causing you to drop the prototype on the floor. You are exasperated and want to withdraw, but the producer insists you pitch. Five minutes later, you walk into the studio with your trembling hands starting to sweat. You are about to introduce yourself when Frank utters, "What's that on your hands?" You reply, "This is EcoSparkle." Frank interrupts, mentioning the enormous potential market for temporary decorations and events. The room falls silent as Frank instantly makes you an offer, which you accept. You made Shark Tank history!

Reflection Questions

1. How does this innovative pitching scenario make you feel? Can you identify the emotions that arise as you imagine yourself pitching on Shark Tank?

2. Consider how cerebral courage might help you in this scenario. How could embracing disruption and fostering innovation, despite potential rejection, change your experience of this situation?

3. Think about a time when you've had to present an unconventional idea in your own life. How did cerebral courage help you overcome the challenge?

Applying Cerebral Courage: Two Scenarios

Now that you've considered the concept of cerebral courage through the EcoSparkle pitch scenario let's apply it to real-life situations using the PACE framework: Purpose, Action, Confidence, and Excellence. Below are two scenarios to help you practice using cerebral courage to transform challenges.

Scenario 1: Proposing an unconventional solution at work

Purpose: Recognise your inner drive for innovation and problem-solving. Let this motivation fuel your courage to present unconventional ideas.

Action: Take immediate steps to develop and refine your unconventional solution. Research thoroughly, anticipate potential objections, and prepare a compelling presentation. Schedule a meeting with decision-makers to pitch your idea.

Confidence: As you prepare and present your unconventional solution, notice how your confidence grows. Each step reinforces your ability to think creatively and potentially inspires others to do the same.

Excellence: Reflect on how you handled the presentation and identify areas for improvement. Perhaps you could enhance your public speaking skills or deepen your understanding of the problem you're addressing. Use this experience to continually refine your approach to proposing innovative ideas.

Scenario 2: Launching a unique start-up or side business

Answer the following questions to apply the PACE framework to your situation:

PURPOSE:

- *What unconventional business idea are you considering launching?*
- *Why is pursuing this innovative concept important to you?*

COURAGE

- What broader societal or environmental values are you upholding with this business idea?

ACTION:

- What small, manageable step could you take today to develop your unconventional business idea?
- How can you break down the launch process into actionable steps?
- How will you hold yourself accountable for pursuing this innovative idea?

CONFIDENCE:

- After taking your first step towards launching your business, how did you feel?
- What positive self-talk can you use to reinforce your decision to pursue this unconventional idea?
- In what ways do you notice your confidence growing as you face the challenges of launching an innovative business?

EXCELLENCE:

- What long-term goal can you set for your unconventional business?
- How can you use any setbacks or skepticism as learning opportunities?
- How might pursuing this unconventional business idea contribute to your growth and industry?

Remember to approach these questions with honesty and self-compassion. Your journey of developing moral courage is unique, and every step forward, no matter how small, is progress.

WRAP UP

What would life be like today if we had no mobile phones and used typewriters instead of computers? Cerebral courage is the friend of innovation and cousin of creativity. It empowers us to challenge the status quo, think critically, and pursue transformative ideas.

By embracing cerebral courage, you can turn bold ideas into reality. Whether in your personal life, business, or career, cerebral courage enables you to tunnel through boulders, shining a light on your vision. It provides **clarity, instils confidence, and garners the support you need.**

What ideas do you have for the future? How will you boldly act on them?

My three key learnings:

1. Cerebral courage involves the boldness to embrace disruption, foster innovation, and drive change, often requiring us to challenge established norms.
2. History shows us the profound impact of intellectual bravery.
3. Kilted courage is a special personal memory.

What are your three learnings?

BREAK TIME

Before proceeding to the second half of the book, take a moment to pause, reflect, and **consider all the times you have been courageous.**

We all have brave memories that can help us overcome fear and make better decisions. I call this process the **"courage bank."** The power of courage is immense and can help us achieve remarkable feats.

During a job interview, you may be asked to share stories of courage. You probably use the STAR method (Situation, Task, Action, Result). You describe the problems you faced, your actions to solve them, how you overcame obstacles and the outcomes you achieved. **Your actions and results showcase your success. You are the star of your own story**. Courage can transport you to a library of opportunity filled with books of success.

What ideas do you have for the future? How will you boldly act on them?

Courage Bank Exercise

Become the STAR of YOUR STORY and write down one memory for each pillar of courage:

1. **Emotional Courage:** The willingness to open up to a broad spectrum of emotions.

    Memory:

2. **Physical Courage**: Acting bravely in the face of fear or pain.

    Memory:

3. **Moral Courage:** Taking a firm stand for what you believe in and committing to your values.

   Memory:

4. **Empathetic courage:** Understanding others, practising humility, and setting aside personal bias.

   Memory:

5. **Steadfast Courage:** Being resolute, focused, and purposeful.

   Memory:

6. **Cerebral Courage:** Disruption, innovation, and driving change.

   Memory:

In March 2019, the word "courage" was tattooed on my back to commemorate my journey. I'm not afraid of needles, but the tattoo gun putting permanent ink close to my bones was painful. It felt like a swarm of bees collecting nectar from an orchard of octopus trees squirting ink, rewarding bravery. The experience **imprinted courage on my backbone and in my mind.** When I asked the tattooist how much longer it would take, he said, "Half an hour," but finished two minutes later. We couldn't help but laugh when he said, "All done." Courage was now part of my DNA. **It was a habit.**

Employing Courage as a Habit: Five Steps

1. **Start from a place of courage:** Practise self-care, find and be a role model.

2. **Lean into Fear:** Pay attention to how it shows up, stay present and connect with the truth.

3. **Commit to your values:** Do the right thing, not what is easy, and stand firm for your beliefs.

4. **Make courage the norm**: Accept where others are at and their mistakes and use positive language to boost confidence.

5. **Be Consistent:** Don't just keep thinking; decide to deliver and get on with it!

"*Friendship is the hardest thing in the world to explain. It's not something you learn in school. But if you haven't learned the meaning of friendship, you really haven't learned anything.*" — Muhammad Ali.

You have learnt the meaning and the six pillars of courage. Now let's make courage a habit and your best friend!

CHAPTER SEVEN

A PLACE OF COURAGE

CHAPTER SEVEN

Start from a place of Courage

HOW DO YOU APPROACH TRYING A NEW TASK?

Training wheels, also known as stabilisers outside North America and Australia, are the extra set of wheels attached to the rear wheel of a bicycle. They are the safety blanket that helps beginners learn to ride independently. The bicycle effectively becomes a tricycle. At some point, the safety blanket is thrown away. The tricycle is now a courageous cycle, with bravery as the extra wheels. Stepping on the pedals creates a mixture of hesitation and anticipation, where excitement dilutes fear. Pedals wobble beneath your feet, and the bike feels slightly unsteady, causing you to pause, learn and adapt.

Realising the handlebars are too high and the seat is too low, you adjust both and decide to try again. Your hands tightly grip the handlebars, and you notice the seat is slightly uncomfortable. You find your balance and steer the bike in the right direction, relaxing your hands as your grip becomes more confident. Courage pushes you through the initial unease and apprehension. You pick up the pace, focusing on enjoying the ride and looking forward to cycling with your mates.

Linda Wasmer Andrews published an article in May 2015 about how bicycling can sharpen thinking and improve mood. It mentioned:

- *Pedalling a bike helps build a better brain, structurally and functionally.*
- *Cycling outdoors helps reduce stress and decrease symptoms of depression and anxiety.*

COURAGE

- *Pedalling regularly increases the integrity of white matter fibre tracts in the brain.*[15]

The mechanics of a bicycle can be confusing because changing gears adds another layer of complexity. With each ride, you become more attuned to when and how to change gears, grasping the skill through practice and persistence. Riding on the open road is a test of bravery. It can be intimidating with unpredictable traffic, but it's also a place for freedom, independence, and a powerful lesson in self-belief.

Courage propels you forward, teaching you to navigate and trust in your abilities.

WHAT IS STARTING FROM A PLACE OF COURAGE?

Starting from a place of courage involves prioritising your health and well-being. You can't help someone else with their oxygen mask if you can't breathe yourself. Self-care builds a foundation of strength and resilience in your everyday life. You inspire others by modelling behaviours you want them to emulate. You set an example for others through your actions, such as mentoring a younger colleague, sharing your opinions, engaging in challenging conversations, or speaking out. Courage isn't just about big heroic acts but also our everyday choices to live authentically and support others.

This involves setting healthy boundaries to create respectful relationships. It is being comfortable saying "no", even if it disappoints others. Starting from a place of courage requires taking responsibility for mistakes and accountability for personal growth by saying "yes" to the right opportunities. **This level of bravery fosters an environment of trust and authenticity.**

---

[15] Linda Wasmer Andrews "Bicycling Can Sharpen Your Thinking and Improve Your Mood" (Psychology Today May 26, 2015) https://www.psychologytoday.com/intl/blo g/minding-the-body/201505/bicycling-can-sharpen-your-thinking-and-improve-your- mood

Muhammad Ali's Example

Muhammad Ali is my hero. His achievements in and out of the ring are equally inspiring. He is iconic in boxing and the broader context of civil rights and social justice.

History informs the present. Conversations of the past reflect the attitudes of that time and how entrenched prejudice was then. Those same prejudices permeated generations, creating barriers that trailblazers fought to remove.

Michael Parkinson is from Yorkshire, in Northern England. Ironically, having a Northern accent would have prevented Michael from having a significant media career before the 1960s, but attitudes changed. Having a Northern accent became cool and no longer a barrier. Parkinson interviewed Muhammad Ali several times. One interview from 1974 is a powerful example of **what it means to start from a place of courage.**[16]

Speaking out against racism and challenging the status quo appeared to make Parkinson and some of the audience uneasy. In the interview, a member of the audience mentions there are Black and White members of the English boxing team. He asks Ali why he is dividing and not uniting people. Parkinson did not challenge the audience member and seemed to agree with him.

Ali did not waver! He refused to give in to this polite form of English, putting down, "You are causing the problem". That subtle form of bullying adds boulders to the barriers. "It would be much easier if you stopped mentioning the issue and accepted the status quo." Ali's impeccable and unstoppable courage in the face of such disrespect is a constant inspiration.

This moment encapsulates a form of prejudice that often goes unchallenged. The idea is that those who speak out against injustice are themselves causing division. This tactic attempts to shift blame from

---

16 https://www.youtube.com/watch?v=xL98xQEkEWs

issues onto those brave enough to name and confront them. Ali's refusal to bow to this pressure demonstrates the true nature of courage and **willingness to speak truth to power, even when it makes others uncomfortable.**

Ali's bravery in standing up to racism is a powerful example of what it means to start from a place of courage. He expressed wisdom when he said, *"Don't count the days; make the days count."*

THE START OF THE WORLD GAY BOXING CHAMPIONSHIPS

Courage to Share my Message

Would you take the opportunity to join the top 1% for free?

One random conversation sparked a thousand conversations, tens of thousands of connections, and tens of millions of impressions. In April 2019, I had no job and needed a break. Let's call it a sabbatical – a period of reflection and reinvigoration. Sitting next to an acquaintance on the bus, she mentioned using LinkedIn to attract clients. It had changed from a career platform into a vital hub for business. She said I needed to be on there.

Brave people share their thoughts to enhance their influence.

Arriving home, I created a LinkedIn account and started exploring the platform, discovering that only 1% of users regularly posted content. As I saw it, 99% of the members left 99% of the opportunities to the 1%. I decided to be part of the 1%! With its professional yet approachable vibe, LinkedIn was the perfect platform for me. Professionals not in stuffy pinstriped suits provided valuable advice, **connecting and engaging with their audience and building rapport.** Women were breaking through the glass ceiling and sharing their messages. I knew creating content on LinkedIn **meant disregarding any fears about what others might think of me.** This was a fortuitous move. It opened up new job opportunities. My message and content were everywhere in the first few months. None of this mattered. I wasn't scared to put myself out there and share my thoughts.

A boxer who never enters the ring automatically forfeits the match.

As I continued creating content, people saw my potential and became friends. My message sharpened and initially focused on procurement, writing articles, and recording videos. This increased my visibility and reputation and expanded my network globally. Within three months, I was invited to be a podcast guest, and journalists interviewed me to tap into my expertise. I attended networking events and met LinkedIn connections in person.

Sharing my Passion and Purpose

I shared videos of my boxing training and my ambition to compete at the Gay Games and secure a gold medal for Australia. This led to the creation of the cheeky moniker "Future World Gay Boxing Champion." A month or so later, there was a crucial discovery: boxing wasn't on the list of sports for the Gay Games. This sparked an idea that would change the course of my journey – why not create the World Gay Boxing Championships (WGBC)?

This could lead to solving one of the biggest problems in sports: homophobia.

LGBTQ+ sporting events had been taking place for over 40 years, but there had never been a world boxing championship for the LGBTQ+ community and its allies. **There was a need.**

A study conducted by Out on the Fields showing 80% of people in Australia have either witnessed or experienced homophobia in sport, with 75% believing that an openly gay person would not be safe as a spectator at a sporting event.[17] Sport is a well-known intervention strategy that boosts confidence and improves mental and physical health outcomes.

---

17 https://outonthefields.com/media/

At the time, LinkedIn was testing a new feature enabling a few users to broadcast live videos on the platform. My application was approved, and I was among the first Australians to be granted this sought-after opportunity. I started a weekly show, "The Courage Panel", **sharing my story, vision and message with the professional and business world.** I discussed the World Gay Boxing Championships and became an advocate for combating homophobia in sports and standing up for the LGBTQ+ community. This led to new friendships and expanded my influence to the next level, **with people offering to help me realise my dream.**

The Courage Champion and the WGBC Board

One of the best ways to counter a culture of fear is to model bravery and communicate a simple, straightforward, consistent message of courage. The word champion is preferable to the word winner. Champions **champion the cause of others, supporting and helping them succeed in their goals and encouraging them to win.** People frequently said I was a role model and inspired courage, which led to my handle, **"The Courage Champion."** Boldly communicating my Big Hairy Audacious Goal (BHAG) created a collective voice for inclusion and positive change. This helped me triumph over trolling and online bullying, which was sometimes relentless.

*I want to say a **big thank you from the bottom of my heart** to everyone who has supported WGBC and me: the many **wondrous people and compassionate allies** on LinkedIn and at networking events.*

I met the WGBC Board on LinkedIn and networking events and want to acknowledge my sincere gratitude and appreciation publicly:

Jenny Vaz extended the hand of friendship when I was unsure about creating content on LinkedIn. She validated my confidence, and in return, I told her that she would make a perfect COO. She is. Her digital expertise added magic to the WGBC website and social media. Jenny built a community of boxers and has bucketloads of courage and laughter.

Flavia de Souza invited me to her networking event in Sydney, and we became friends instantly. She became my lawyer, helping me through a turbulent period and achieving a significant outcome. Flavia enabled WGBC to become a registered business and obtain the trademark. She inspired me to be courageous when my depression was at its worst. Her legal, business, and life advice is as good as the walks we enjoy.

Sharon White was there for me when I struggled to address a significant problem. She was my guide and stood by me most when I needed help. We became instant friends. Her strategic advice, approach, and extensive project experience are precious. She makes the best Christmas dinner in the world, and I'll be brave and say that her roast potatoes are better than my mum's.

Paul Johnston brought his expertise, experience, and big heart to every moment and conversation. He is an excellent CFO to have by your side. Paul sees the enormity of opportunity and writes the best business plans to make it happen. I love meeting up for coffee with Paul and having great conversations with him.

Remember my definition of courage: take ownership of fear and venture forward with confidence and resilience. The WGBC Board exemplify courage.

WHAT CAN WE LEARN FROM THE SMALLEST CROCODILES?

The Unexpected Benefits of Facing Fears

Crocodiles are nature's survivors. They remain resilient as the earth goes through periods of harmony, then rack, and sadly, ruin. Their stopwatch started from a place of courage and recorded unlimited laps of bravery. The West African dwarf crocodile is a small, nocturnal species found in the rainforests and swamps of West Africa. It is also the smallest crocodile species.

COURAGE

While kayaking across a crocodile pond in Ghana, the guide pointed to a small island where flocks of birds nested. He explained the birds' symbiotic relationship with the snappy reptiles. The crocs keep the birds safe and away from danger. The neighbourhood has cobras, puff adders, pythons, and other predators. *Would you prefer a viper or Tyrannosaurus Rex's aquatic cousins living next door?*

While the crocodiles pose a potential threat, they also offer protection from other predators. The snakes pose a more immediate danger to the birds and their offspring. This isn't exactly "the enemy of my enemy is my friend." The crocs create a more balanced ecosystem. Swimming serpents with a tummy rumbling make a more wholesome meal than a nestling. It's like a jumbo burger and fries compared to a hash brown or a supersized serving instead of a bite-sized snack.

What appears threatening at first glance (the crocodiles) can provide security when viewed in a broader context. It serves as a reminder that **courage sometimes means looking beyond our initial fears.** This arrangement benefits the crocodiles. The presence of the birds provides them with potential food sources, both in terms of the birds themselves and the smaller prey animals attracted to the nesting areas.

Starting from a place of courage involves prioritising safety.

Australia has some of the world's largest crocodiles, and they are potentially dangerous. Some of Douglas Shire Council's advice on being Croc-Wise can be applied to everyday life, including:

- *Never take unnecessary risks in crocodile habitat. You are responsible for your safety.*
- *Obey crocodile warning signs – they are there for your safety and protection.*
- *Never provoke, harass or interfere with crocodiles, even small ones.*[18]

---

18 https://douglas.qld.gov.au/croc-wise/

Start from a place of Courage

How can you Learn Croc Ecosystem

The relationship between the crocodiles and the birds nesting near them illustrates a complex interplay of risk and safety. At first glance, it might seem counterintuitive for birds to choose to nest in such proximity to predators. However, this **choice demonstrates a form of calculated courage** that ultimately enhances their chances of survival.

The lesson is clear: courage isn't about the absence of fear but about making strategic choices in the face of it. Sometimes, the path that seems **most frightening at first can be the one that offers the best security and opportunity for growth.**

Here are six key learnings you can draw from the fascinating crocodile and bird symbiotic relationship:

1. **Unexpected alliances can provide safety:** The birds nesting near the crocodiles teach us that safety can sometimes come from unexpected sources. In life and business, forming alliances with those who might initially seem threatening can offer protection from other, more immediate dangers.

2. **Calculated risks can lead to greater security:** By choosing to nest near crocodiles, birds take a calculated risk that enhances their safety. They are following their instincts. This reminds us that sometimes, what appears risky at first glance can provide greater security when viewed in a broader context.

3. **Perspective changes everything:** What seems dangerous from one perspective (e.g., crocodiles to birds) can be beneficial from another (e.g., protection from snakes). This teaches us the importance of looking at situations from multiple angles before making judgments or decisions.

4. **Mutual benefit can arise from unlikely situations:** The crocodiles benefit from the birds' presence, just as the birds benefit from the crocodiles' presence. This symbiotic relationship shows how seemingly opposed parties can find ways to coexist that benefit both.

COURAGE

5. **Courage often involves choosing between known and unknown risks:** The birds' choice to nest near crocodiles rather than risk snake attacks illustrates how courage sometimes means choosing a known risk over an unknown one. In our lives, we might need to face familiar challenges head-on rather than risk unfamiliar dangers.

6. **Nature provides models for complex problem-solving:** The ecosystem at the crocodile pond demonstrates how complex problems can be solved through natural balance and adaptation. This can inspire us to look for holistic, systemic solutions to our challenges, considering how different elements can work together for the overall benefit.

COURAGE IN ACTION

On 26 January 1926, John Logie Baird (yes, the Logies! A tribute to Baird) boldly unveiled authentic television images to the esteemed members of the Royal Institution and a discerning reporter from The Times. In an era when television was a mere figment of the imagination, Baird fearlessly pursued what many deemed an impossible task. Envision the pressure of showcasing this groundbreaking invention to a journalist from the most influential media company in the country. Picture the eminent figures from the scientific world **eagerly anticipating Baird's success or failure.**

His journey to this historic moment was fraught with challenges. Baird faced skepticism from the scientific community, financial difficulties, and numerous technical obstacles. **He worked tirelessly, often in less-than-ideal conditions,** to develop the necessary components for his television system. Using makeshift equipment such as a tea chest, bicycle lamp, and a scanning disk, Baird assembled a rudimentary yet functional apparatus that could transmit live images.

On a cold January day in his laboratory in Soho, London, the journalist and a small group of scientists witnessed Baird making history. As the first flickering images appeared on the screen, **the audience was astonished by what they saw:** a live, moving image transmitted over the airwaves.

Despite the risk of failure, Baird's bravery in presenting his invention to the world sparked technological capability and innovation. It reshaped society and radically shifted how people accessed, consumed, and enjoyed entertainment in the decades ahead. His determination and bravery paved the way for the modern television era. **It changed the way we communicate and experience the world.**

Exercise: Croc Challenge – Taming the Dental Dilemma

OBJECTIVE: *Embracing challenges for growth*

This exercise aims to help you start from a place of courage when facing fears to:

1. Develop empathy for others facing fear and anxiety in everyday situations.
2. Use humour and personal connection to ease tension and build trust.
3. Recognise the power of being a supportive presence in challenging moments.
4. Explore creative problem-solving techniques when conventional approaches fall short.
5. Build confidence in your ability to influence others' experiences positively.
6. Reflect on personal courage experiences and how they can be applied to help others.

This exercise assists in developing courage, supportive behaviour, problem-solving skills, and emotional intelligence.

Imaginary Scene

The Ghanaian crocodiles invite you to their Australian relatives. The Aussie Crocs, with their ferocious reputation, are considered the most dangerous in the world. The Ghana crew told you about their legendary Uncle Bert and Auntie Doris. Bert, a character who breaks wind, burps, and tells dirty jokes in the pub, is always in hot water when Doris gives him a disapproving stare and shrieks, "Albert". Doris works full-time as CEO of Croc Bank, ensuring she has time for family and friends on weekends.

You meet Bert at the dentist. He has a toothache and is petrified of opening wide while the drill relieves his pain. Doris booked the appointment and confirmed the booking by saying, "Albert, you need to go." Bert is trembling, with sweat running down his scales. He wants to run through the door, but you must stop him. You promised Doris to take care of him. You try to explain that there is nothing to be frightened of. You say, "Think of the poor dentist having to clean your foul mouth." Memories of mucky jokes and rude one-liners over rounds of beer with his mates start Bert's giggles. This was only a temporary relief as the dentist called his name.

You accompany Bert into the dentist's room as he leans back in the chair. The dentist picks up the mouth mirror to view Bert's teeth and the sickle probe to detect cavities in his snappers. Bert's claws are pale white. You believe he is about to flee when the dentist asks him to open wide. The dentist quips, "Did you hear the one about...?" It was a joke Bert would be proud to tell his mates. Bert doesn't need laughing gas; he relaxes and trusts the dentist to do his job. Twenty minutes later, Bert smiles with a bag of jellybeans and makes an appointment for his next dental check-up.

Reflection Questions

1. How did you feel about Bert's initial fear of the dentist, and in what ways can you relate to his anxiety?

2. What emotions did you experience when you successfully helped Bert relax through humour and support?

3. How do you think this experience might change Bert's perspective on future dental visits, and what lessons can you draw from this for your own life challenges?

For each of the six pillars of courage, identify a personal memory that demonstrates that type of courage. Reflect on how these memories can help you face future challenges and be a role model for others, especially in situations like assisting Bert in overcoming his fear of the dentist.

Start from a place of Courage

Scenario 1: Helping a Friend Overcome Fear of Driving (Example)

Emotional Courage Memory: Opening up to a friend about anxiety when they start driving and sharing vulnerable feelings to create a connection.

Physical Courage Memory: Sitting in the passenger seat during a friend's first driving lesson, despite your nervousness about being in a car with a new driver.

Moral Courage Memory: Gently but firmly insist your friend follow traffic rules during practice, even when they want to take shortcuts.

Empathetic Courage Memory: Truly listen to your friend's fears about driving without dismissing them or rushing to offer solutions, allowing them to feel heard and understood.

Steadfast Courage Memory: Consistently make time for driving practice sessions with your friend, even when you're busy or the weather is poor.

Cerebral Courage Memory: Researching and suggesting an innovative approach to learning driving skills, such as using a driving simulator before getting on the road.

Scenario 2: Helping a Friend Overcome a Fear (Your Turn)

Think about when you needed to help a friend face a fear. Use the Courage Bank concept to identify memories that can help you be a supportive and courageous friend. Fill in your memories for each type of courage:

Emotional Courage: The willingness to open up to a broad spectrum of emotions.

Memory:

Physical Courage: Acting bravely in the face of fear or pain.

Memory:

COURAGE

Moral Courage: Taking a firm stand for what you believe in and committing to your values.

Memory:

Empathetic Courage: Understanding others, practising humility, and setting aside personal bias.

Memory:

Steadfast Courage: Being resolute, focused, and purposeful.

Memory:

Cerebral Courage: Disruption, innovation, and driving change

Memory:

Remember to approach these questions with honesty and self-compassion. Your development journey is unique, and every step forward, no matter how small, is progress.

WRAP UP

Starting from a place of courage is the foundation upon which all other brave acts are built. It's not about waiting for the courage to find us but actively cultivating it as our default starting point. This proactive approach to bravery transforms how we face each day, each challenge, and each interaction.

Start from a place of Courage

It's about **making courage your first step**, not your last resort. In doing so, you don't just change your trajectories; **you create ripples of bravery and forge new paths for others to follow**.

Be patient with yourself as you grow and celebrate the moments when you successfully **connect with others on a deeper level.** Your efforts in **developing empathetic courage will benefit those around yo**u and enrich your life experiences.

My three key learnings:

1. Starting from a place of courage is a conscious choice that requires self-care, authenticity, and a willingness to be vulnerable.

2. As Muhammad Ali and the creation of WGBC demonstrated, Courage in communication can challenge societal norms and create platforms for positive change.

3. Building a support network of courageous individuals, like the WGBC Board, can amplify your impact and help you overcome obstacles in pursuing your goals.

What are your three learnings?

CHAPTER EIGHT

LEAN INTO FEAR

CHAPTER EIGHT
Lean into Fear

WHEN DO YOU TAKE A LEAP OF FAITH?

The idiom "Taking the Plunge" refers to committing yourself to a bold action. You might feel nervous about moving into something uncertain or challenging, but it involves overcoming hesitation and embracing the unknown with confidence and exuberance.

The 3-meter springboard is a flexible diving board that uses elasticity to help divers gain height and momentum for intricate flips and twists. Divers must maintain precise control over their movements, as even a slight miscalculation can affect their entry angle and overall score. The 10-meter platform, in contrast, is rigid and non-flexible, from which divers jump directly. This height can present a gargantuan psychological and physical challenge. Standing on the platform, the distance from the diver's eyes to the bottom of the diving pit can be 17 metres. Divers must conquer any fear of heights or the consequences of a misstep. The height requires divers to execute their routines with precise timing and technique. The impact with the water is much more significant than from the 3-meter board.

By pushing through a challenge like leaping off a 10-metre platform, you add a new dimension to your character. This growth is not just about conquering fear, but also about inspiring and motivating yourself to reach new heights.

Douglas LaBier Ph.D. published an article in May 2019 highlighting the following ways you can consciously grow previously undeveloped dimensions:

- Identify qualities within you that you believe exist but have remained dormant and want to strengthen.
- Visualise embodying that quality in your daily life. Describe the expanded version of yourself.
- Reflect on what you must do daily to strengthen that dimension as if you're developing a new habit.
- Imagine a tether attached to the qualities you want to evolve, pulling you steadily upward towards them.
- Reflect on what you must do daily to strengthen those dimensions as if you are building new muscles.[19]

Olympic divers improve by adopting the ethos of 'The School of Hard Knocks.' They learn valuable lessons through training in one of the Games' most captivating and challenging events. These lessons arise from repeated jumps, twists and turns, building resilience and character. These experiences shape how they become skillful and talented divers, instilling in them a sense of determination and persistence.

Diving from these heights demands mental fortitude and physical strength.

WHAT IS LEANING INTO FEAR?

Leaning into fear means paying attention to how it shows up, staying present and connecting with the truth. It allows you to determine the ways fear manifests. This unexpected and potentially dangerous feeling can become harmful when you avoid confronting it. When you acknowledge the truth, fear can guide you towards making better decisions.

Just as teachers encourage us to listen in school to learn, understand, ask questions, and enhance our knowledge, facing our fears head-on is vital for personal growth. Being too afraid to ask a question is a missed opportunity. It might take time and effort to recover, consuming valuable resources you could use for something more productive. High jumpers

---

[19] https://www.psychologytoday.com/au/blog/the-new-resilience/201905/want-greater-mental-health-plunge-forward-the-unknown

succeed when the bar is set higher. **Progress is hindered when you allow fear to hold you back.**

A quivering crab retreats into its protective shell. This cautious beachcomber emerges only when the tranquil waves of safety wash away the turbulent tides of fear. It carefully scans its surroundings for threats. The crab tempers its anxiety, skillfully avoiding the grasp of danger. Instinctively, the crab stays hidden beneath its sandy cloak, guided by wise caution that protects it from harm. Yet, when the moment calls for courage, it boldly steps out of its shell. It is ready to face the world. With each determined claw, it navigates the shoreline, embracing exploration risks.

Courage is always discoverable in our world of fear.

Junko Tabei's Example

Junko Tabei was a Japanese mountaineer, author, and teacher. Her love for mountain climbing began at age ten during a class climbing trip to Mount Nasu. She cherished the sport's non-competitive nature and enjoyed the breathtaking natural landscapes from the mountain's summit.

Born in 1939 in a Japan that held traditional views on women's roles, Tabei defied societal expectations by pursuing dangerous and physically demanding activities, **undeterred by the fear of being judged or ostracised**. Tabei's decision to form The Ladies Climbing Club in 1969 was a bold step. It challenged the male-dominated climbing community in Japan. The club's motto was "Let's go on an overseas expedition by ourselves," reflecting her commitment to empowering women in mountaineering.

The 1975 Everest expedition tested Tabei's courage and resourcefulness. She was confronted with significant financial constraints that could have derailed the project. She took on additional work as a teacher to raise funds and participated in radio and television interviews. She even crafted waterproof pouches for calendars to sell, **showcasing her resourcefulness and unwavering determination.**

During the climb, Tabei faced a near-death experience when an avalanche struck their camp. Buried under snow, she was unconscious for approximately six minutes before being dug out by Sherpas. Many would have abandoned the climb after such a traumatic event, but she continued the ascent. On May 16, 1975, Tabei reached the summit of Everest, becoming the first woman to do so.

But Tabei didn't stop there. She continued to climb the highest peaks on every continent, becoming the first woman to complete the Seven Summits. This a feat that requires considerable endurance, skill, and mental strength. This achievement **was a personal triumph and a powerful statement.**

She literally and figuratively demonstrated the ability to reach great heights.

ADVOCATING FOR INCLUSION WITH RESILIENCE

Fear to Solve a Major Problem

Kindness attracts kindness. Bravery attracts bravery; impeccable courage attracts courageous people to help you. **Individuals don't fear succeeding when they have excellent people by their side**.

All that glitters is not gold.

Glossy statements about inclusion and diversity are meaningless unless backed up with authentic actions.

Sprinkling glitter on boxing gloves will not daze an opponent. Scratch beneath the surface, and all you have are boxing gloves. The peregrine falcon is renowned worldwide for its agility and resilience. It's respected for its courage and steadfastness, nurturing its chicks in a secure, moral environment. **These behaviours embody the values and spirit of sport.**

Imagine the head of Diversity, Equity, and Inclusion (DEI) at a prestigious private school giving an interview to the local newspaper. He proudly declares the institution's support for all communities. However, their words rang hollow as no tangible actions were taken to address the pressing issues. I reached out for an update, hoping for real progress. I was ignored, with emails not replied to and unfollowed on social media. This cut off any avenue for further dialogue.

The school principal frequently touts a commitment to creating an inclusive, anti-bullying culture in the school's annual statements. However, when influential families whose children are involved in bullying express their displeasure, the principal quietly abandons the anti-bullying stance. He chooses to ignore the issue. Instead of showing the strength and integrity of a peregrine falcon, the principal behaves more like an ostrich, burying his head in the sand.

A substantive effort is needed to stop the foe of hatred from winning round after round.

The superficial approach not only fails to address the root causes of homophobia but also perpetuates an environment where discrimination can thrive unchallenged. Actual progress requires more than just glittering promises and polished mission statements. It demands courage, consistency, and a willingness to face opposition. We need organisations that stand firm in their commitments and **whose authentic efforts create a genuinely inclusive environment in sports and beyond.**

The Real Deal

My experience with Boxing Australia and Boxing NSW stands out as a beacon of hope and genuine allyship. I approached Boxing Australia, seeking their support. From the outset, a meaningful and collaborative relationship was established.

I experienced a warm welcome into the Australian boxing family.

I had two meetings with Boxing Australia. Within two weeks, the Board pledged to support WGBC and promised to provide all the guidance and institutional assistance we needed. This swift and decisive action demonstrated a commitment that went beyond mere words.

COURAGE

Boxing New South Wales (NSW) was equally fabulous in its support. Sean Fitzpatrick, the President of Boxing NSW, invited me to a boxing club in Sydney. I walked into the gym with a welcome as warm as Nan's apple and blackberry pie. **Friendships were forged in seconds.**

I joined the class and enjoyed the three rounds of skipping. I usually skip the skipping and warm-up on a bike or rowing machine instead, but this warm-up was extra special. We went for coffee afterwards. Sean promised he and Boxing NSW would be with us every step of the way. They were! This level of personal engagement and **genuine interest in our cause was refreshing and inspiring.**

Boxing Australia and Boxing NSW extended their support beyond mere pleasantries. They actively collaborated with us, offering their expertise, resources, and platforms to amplify our message. We collaborated on a press release announcing Boxing Australia's support for WGBC. **This collaboration increased the visibility and credibility of our cause.**

Their unwavering support exemplified true allyship in action. It wasn't just about making statements or ticking boxes; it was about actively working together to create a more inclusive boxing community. This partnership demonstrated how established organisations can use their influence and resources to support emerging initiatives promoting inclusion. **It showed what institutions can achieve.**

I cannot thank my friends at Boxing Australia and Boxing NSW enough. You epitomise allyship and exemplify boxing's values

Their actions serve as a model for how sports organisations can effectively support and promote inclusivity, setting a standard for others to follow.

Leadership Extinguishing the Firestorm

My journey took an unexpected turn after contacting The Guardian newspaper. They interviewed me and published a splendid article encapsulating WGBC's purpose and Boxing Australia's remarkable support. I thought there might be some **backlash on social media, but not headline news.**

The following morning, a friend in Perth, the capital city of Western Australia, sent me a message. A prominent politician who doubled as a television sports commentator and popular radio host mentioned *The Guardian* article on his radio show. The politician made an extremely offensive and derogatory remark about trans people on his radio show. The company sponsoring the radio show distanced itself, issuing a statement condemning the remark.

It was the main news story in Western Australia and was reported in other media outlets across Australia. The politician apologised in front of a packed press release. To his credit, **he promised to educate himself and spend time with the LGBTQ+ community, which he did.**

Leadership was urgently needed.

I tuned into ABC Perth, where the derogatory comments incensed caller after caller. When humans' anger resembles a dormant volcano unexpectedly erupting, calmness and reason are the perfect coolants. I called ABC Perth, explaining I was the Founder and CEO of the World Gay Boxing Championships. WGBC was repeatedly mentioned in the news; it only seemed fitting that we were heard. I condemned the offensive remark and acknowledged the politician's apology. I said it was best to accept the apology, and the matter is now closed. This extinguished the fire instead of fanning the flames.

Some conversations are better held in private.

The Chief of the Fire Department inspects burnt-down buildings to ascertain the cause of the fire. As the CEO, it was my job to examine the firestorm. I emailed the politician, expressing my profound disappointment and explaining how his behaviour undeservedly tarnished WGBC's reputation. **It made the task of disrupting hatred in sports harder.** He apologised profusely, offering to make amends. He invited me to talk about WGBC on his radio show, Perth's most popular.

I was welcomed with the theme tune of the first Rocky movie, and we had a fantastic conversation. It was like chatting with mates over coffee at your favourite cafe. They are genuinely interested in your work, and their excitement about knowing more makes you curious and engaged.

Leadership involves letting go of anger and helping others learn from and overcome their mistakes.

While initially distressing, this incident ultimately provided an opportunity to demonstrate the power of dialogue and education in combating prejudice. By engaging constructively rather than perpetuating anger, we turned a negative situation into a platform for raising awareness and promoting understanding. It highlighted the importance of resilience and strategic thinking in advocacy work. I showed that sometimes the most effective way to combat discrimination is through education.

Allow others the chance to learn and grow.

WHAT CAN WE LEARN FROM NATURE'S HIGH DIVERS?

The Feathered Water Canon

Kingfishers are nature's aquatic acrobats. They are **compact superheroes** with disproportionately large heads. They sport dagger-like bills that are perfect for spearing unsuspecting fish. When it comes to hunting, kingfishers have a signature move. A death-defying plunge from their perch straight into the water below with built-in goggles! They have a transparent third eyelid, called the nictitating membrane, that slides across their eyes underwater. It lets them keep their eyes peeled for prey while protecting them from aquatic debris.

Kingfishers are surprisingly shy and experts at blending in. When viewed from above, their blue backs mimic the water, protecting them from predators. At the first sign of danger, they're off like a shot. Their rattling call serves as both a warning and a signal for a swift exit.

Kingfishers are not just fascinating creatures; **they are integral to their ecosystems.** They're often cultural icons in many societies and examples of nature's ingenuity. From their unique hunting techniques to their devoted parenting, kingfishers continue to inspire and amaze. Their presence in our world is a testament to the fact that sometimes, **the most extraordinary things come in small, feathered packages**.

Birdfact.com provides an extensive description of the birds, mentioning behaviours that humans can learn from:

- *They usually perch just a meter above the surface, preferring still or gently flowing water.*
- *If there is no suitable perch, the kingfisher will hover for several seconds before plunging into the water.*
- *Kingfisher chicks eat fish delivered by both parents. Their first meals are tiny and get progressively larger as their young grow.*[20]

How can you Learn from Kingfishers

Kingfishers, nature's champion divers, offer a **treasure trove of lessons for those willing to observe and learn.** These vibrant birds' remarkable adaptations and behaviours inspire **resilience, precision, and adaptability.** By studying these feathered marvels, you can glean valuable insights. Here are six examples of ways you can learn from kingfishers:

1. **Precision and Focus:** Kingfishers demonstrate the power of laser-like concentration in achieving goals. Their ability to spot and accurately dive for fish teaches us the importance of maintaining focus and acting decisively when opportunities arise.

2. **Adaptability:** These birds thrive in various habitats, from tropical forests to urban waterways, showcasing the value of flexibility. Humans can learn to adapt to changing environments and circumstances, finding success in diverse situations.

---

20 https://birdfact.com/birds/kingfisher

3. **Patience and Timing:** Kingfishers often wait motionless for the perfect moment to strike, illustrating the virtues of patience and strategic timing. This behaviour reminds us that success usually comes to those who wait for the right moment and act swiftly.

4. **Resourcefulness:** Some kingfisher species have adapted to eat a variety of prey, not just fish, demonstrating resourcefulness. This teaches us the importance of diversifying our skills and being open to alternative solutions when faced with challenges.

5. **Teamwork in Parenting:** Male and female kingfishers share responsibilities in rearing their young, from incubation to feeding. This cooperative approach to parenting offers a model for equitable partnerships and shared responsibilities in human relationships.

6. **Overcoming Fear:** Despite their small size, kingfishers fearlessly dive into water at high speeds to catch their prey. Their courage in the face of potential danger encourages us to confront our fears and take calculated risks to pursue our goals.

COURAGE IN ACTION

The main swimming pool in my hometown of Grimsby was a classic, council-run facility built in the 1960s. It was well-designed and had a 6-lane swimming pool and an adjoining diving bay. I loved the place, but it also scared the life out of me. I swam competitively and trained at the pool two or three times a week.

The maximum depth of the main pool was almost two metres, and the diving bay's depth was around four metres. Swimming over deep water frightened me, so I avoided swimming in the end lanes where you could see the bottom of the diving bay.

The fastest swimmers used to train in the lanes next to the diving bay. Continuing competitive swimming meant keeping my eyes open for two-hour training sessions. **Familiarisation helped me navigate the fear.** Swimming on the left-hand side of the lane was just enough to look slightly away from the diving bay without seeing the depth. Swimming on the right-hand side only required seeing my fear for around 10 seconds. **Putting this into perspective and partial exposure reduced the impact of the fear.**

Relatability was another helpful strategy. When walking or in the family car, I looked for signs showing the height of a bridge, structure, or bus. These items were around four metres and didn't scare me. Envisioning the bottom of the diving bay as looking down from a proper bench or sitting on the top deck of a double-decker bus **desensitised the fear.**

We competed in a competition with participants from other local schools. I was drawn to swim in the lane next to the diving bay in the freestyle heats. Powering through the area next to the diving bay helped me qualify as the fastest swimmer in the final. I won three events that night. The fear became an ally.

Exercise: Diving into Courage – The Topboard Challenge

OBJECTIVE: *Overcoming personal fears and supporting others through theirs*

This exercise aims to help you lean into fear by:

1. Recognising the power of incremental steps in facing fears.
2. Understanding the impact of positive role models and peer support.
3. Acknowledging the mental hurdles involved in confronting fears.
4. Experiencing the rush of accomplishment after overcoming a fear.
5. Learning to support others in their journey to overcome fears.
6. Reflecting on personal growth and increased confidence after facing fears.

This exercise assists in developing courage, supportive behaviour, problem-solving skills, and emotional intelligence.

COURAGE

Imaginary Scene

You're a swimming instructor at a local pool with three diving boards: a 1m and 3m springboard, and a 5m platform known as the Top Board. A new student, Alex, has joined your advanced swimming class. Alex is comfortable in the water but has never used a diving board before.

You start by having Alex jump from the 1m board, which they manage easily after a brief hesitation. Encouraged by this success, you suggest trying the 3m board. Alex is visibly nervous but agrees to try after watching you demonstrate. With your encouragement, Alex makes the jump and immediately wants to do it again, exhilarated by the experience.

The following week, Alex expresses interest in trying Top Board but is clearly apprehensive. You climb the ladder with them, talking through each step. At the top, Alex freezes, looking down at the water. Another instructor, Sam, notices and calls up, "It's not as scary as it looks!" Sam then demonstrates by diving off the board.

Alex is still hesitant. You remind them of their progress on the lower boards and assure them that you'll be in the water below. After a few deep breaths, Alex takes the plunge. They surface with a huge grin, shouting, "That was amazing!" For the rest of the session, Alex can't get enough of Top Board, repeatedly climbing up for more jumps.

Reflection Questions

1. How did you feel watching Alex's journey from the 1m board to conquering Top Board?
2. What role did your support and Sam's demonstration play in Alex's success?
3. How might this experience change Alex's approach to future challenges, and what lessons can you draw from it to help others overcome their fears?

For each of the six pillars of courage, identify a personal memory related to helping someone overcome a fear of heights or water. Reflect on how these memories can help you face future challenges and be a role model for others, especially in situations like assisting Alex in conquering Top Board.

Scenario 1: Helping Someone Overcome Fear of Heights (Example)

Emotional Courage Memory: Sharing past panic attacks about heights with a friend who was nervous about rock climbing creates a safe space for vulnerability.

Physical Courage Memory: Acting as a friend's climbing partner for their first session despite a lingering fear of heights.

Moral Courage Memory: Firmly insisting on proper safety protocols when a friend wanted to skip steps to "get it over with".

Empathetic Courage Memory: Actively listening to a friend's specific climbing fears without dismissing any, acknowledging each concern.

Steadfast Courage Memory: Consistently attending a six-week climbing course with a friend, even on days we felt like quitting.

Cerebral Courage Memory: Introducing innovative visualisation and mindfulness techniques to help a friend mentally prepare for climbing.

Scenario 2: Helping Someone Overcome Stage Fright (Your Turn)

Think about a time when you needed to help someone face their fear of public speaking or performing in front of an audience. Use the Courage Bank concept to identify memories that can help you be a supportive and courageous mentor. Fill in your memories for each type of courage:

Emotional Courage: The willingness to open up to a broad spectrum of emotions.

Memory:

COURAGE

Physical Courage: Acting bravely in the face of fear or pain.

Memory:

Moral Courage: Taking a firm stand for what you believe in and committing to your values.

Memory:

Empathetic Courage: Understanding others, practising humility, and setting aside personal bias.

Memory:

Steadfast Courage: Being resolute, focused, and purposeful.

Memory:

Cerebral Courage: Disruption, innovation, and driving change.

Memory:

Remember to approach these questions with honesty and self-compassion. Your development journey is unique, and every step forward, no matter how small, is progress.

WRAP UP

Leaning into fear is about developing awareness of how anxiety manifests in our lives, remaining present in challenging moments, and connecting with underlying truths. Paying attention to fear's physical, mental, and behavioural manifestations can yield valuable insights.

Staying present lets you **observe fear objectively**, creating space for **rational thinking and intentional action.** Fear is not your enemy but **a guide pointing towards areas of growth.**

Embrace it as a teacher, and you'll find the strength you never knew you had.

My three key learnings:

1. Courage is developed through practice, self-reflection, and incremental challenges, as demonstrated by the Top Board Challenge exercise.

2. Junko Tabei's journey to becoming the first woman to climb Mount Everest exemplifies how leaning into fear and moving past it can lead to groundbreaking achievements and inspire others.

3. Boxing Australia and Boxing NSW's support and allyship highlight the importance of authentic actions and collaborations in creating meaningful change.

What are your three learnings?

CHAPTER NINE

COMMIT TO VALUES

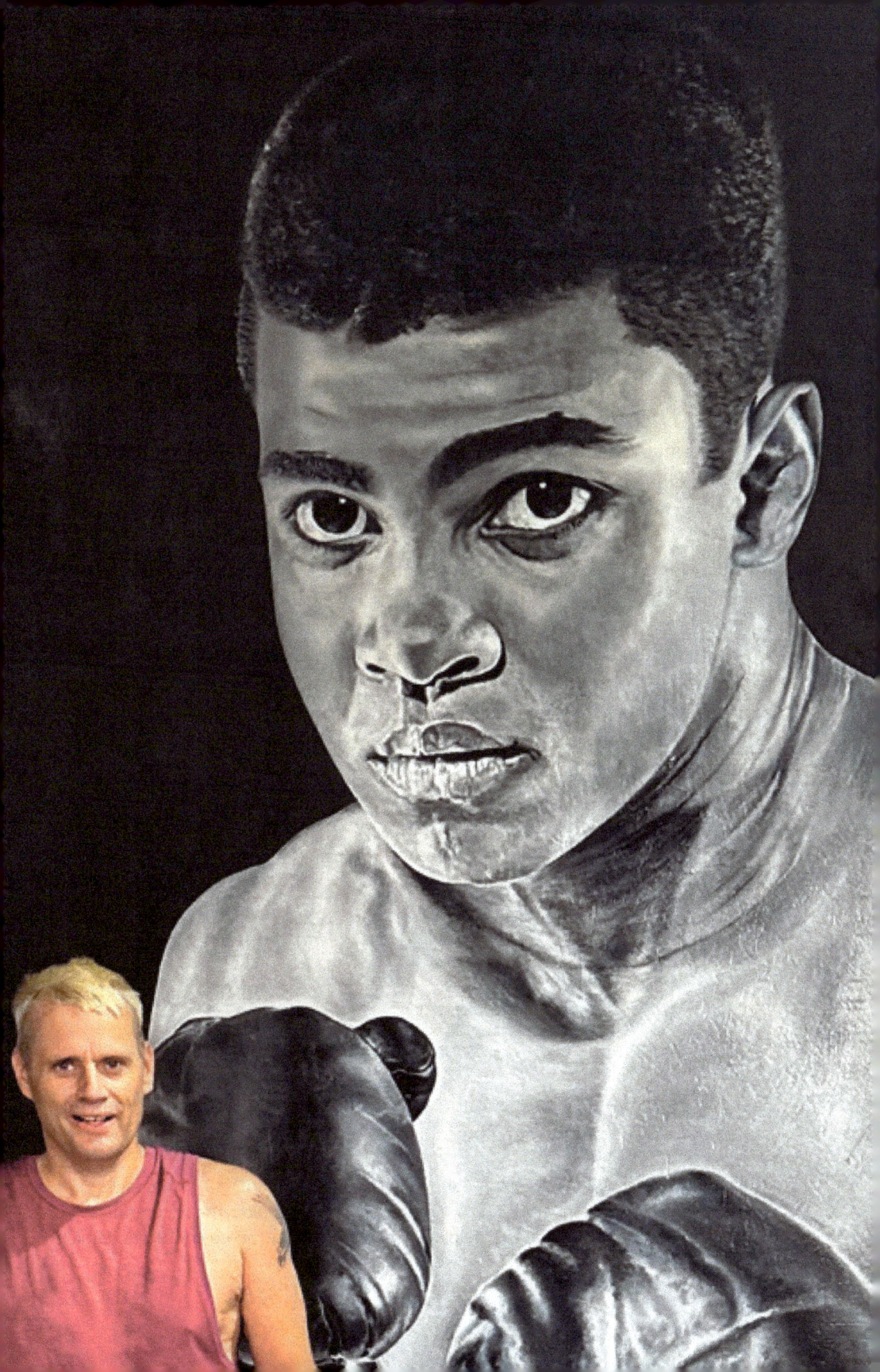

CHAPTER NINE
Committing to Your Values

HOW DO YOU INSPIRE OTHERS TO DO THE RIGHT THING?

During COVID, we had no choice but to adapt. In the first few months of the pandemic, selfishness and recklessness harmed others. Responsibility and humility saved lives and served as a safety net for our emotional and physical health. We tried to support local businesses as they pivoted. It allowed vital community hubs to survive and flourish again after the pandemic. Those important bonds and social connections forged relationships of integrity and bravery.

Inspiring others to do the right thing often begins with leading by example. When we demonstrate responsibility, compassion, and resilience in our actions, it can have a powerful ripple effect on those around us. During the pandemic, those considering others encouraged their communities to do the same.

Prosocial behaviour is behaviour that benefits others or society. Janelle L. Wilson Ph.D. referenced this in her January 2024 article about the COVID-19 Pandemic, highlighting:

- Helping behaviours are especially vital during times of crisis.
- During the COVID-19 pandemic, prosocial behaviour manifests as following public health guidelines.
- In challenging times, helping others can take a variety of forms.[21]

Fostering open and honest communication is essential in inspiring ethical behaviour. By sharing our experiences, challenges, and the positive

---

[21] Janelle L. Wilson Ph.D. "Helping Behaviors During the COVID-19 Pandemic" (Psychology Today, January 23, 2024) https://www.psychologytoday.com/au/blog/stories-of-the-self/202401/helping-behaviors-during-the-covid-19-pandemic

outcomes of our choices, we can motivate others to make similar decisions. It's critical to approach these conversations empathetically and understand that everyone faces unique circumstances. By creating a supportive environment where people feel comfortable discussing their concerns and ideas, we can collaboratively find ways to do the right thing.

It is during challenging times that communities become strong.

WHAT IS COMMITTING TO YOUR VALUES?

Committing to your values by doing what's right isn't easy, but it's essential.

Who said life was easy?

You don't obtain your driver's licence without starting the ignition, looking in the mirror, and driving under supervision hour after hour. The logbook is your record of working towards the goal. You must pass the test to get the licence and follow the rules to keep it.

Penalty points are a deterrent to ensure motorists, passengers, and pedestrians are safe when you are in front of the wheel. When someone complains about receiving a speeding fine after driving 20 km over the speed limit, **were they doing the right thing?** A $200 hit to the wallet is avoidable.

When I was diagnosed with Addison's disease, I had to adapt. Speaking with the "Dalek voice" after the tracheotomy was frustrating. **Giving into despair would have meant having no voice.** People listened to me when I talked like a ventriloquist's toad. They adjusted to me, staying true to their values of common decency. They celebrated when my natural voice returned. It was the same when I came out of the closet. Despite the fear and potential rejection, I accepted my identity. Doing the right thing was much easier than doing the wrong thing, not being me. **Standing firm in my identity and refusing to hide, I honoured my truth and paved the way for others to do the same.**

Despite the challenges, living authentically has been vital to building a life of integrity and purpose. This commitment to values extends beyond personal experiences to every aspect of life, including our professional endeavours and social interactions. **It's about consistently choosing the path of integrity,** even when uncomfortable or unpopular. By doing so, we stay true to ourselves and inspire others to embrace their authentic selves.

This cascade of authenticity can lead to more inclusive, understanding, and compassionate communities.

Sir Matt's Busby's Example

Sir Matt Busby, a Scottish football player and manager, became a legendary figure in the football world, particularly for his tenure at Manchester United. Born in 1909, Busby's love for the beautiful game began in his youth when he played for various clubs before transitioning into management. He was appointed as Manchester United's manager in 1945.

Busby's philosophy **centred on nurturing young talent,** earning his team the moniker "Busby Babes." These young players, many of whom he had personally scouted and developed, formed the core of a team that captured the imagination of fans across England.

However, tragedy struck on February 6, 1958, when the plane carrying the Manchester United team crashed on takeoff in Munich. The disaster claimed the lives of 23 people, including eight players. Busby himself was critically injured, receiving the last rites twice during his two-month hospital stay. The crash devastated the team and sent shockwaves to the football community and beyond.

In the face of this **unimaginable loss, Busby's resilience shone through.** He was determined to honour the memory of those lost by rebuilding the team and leading Manchester United back to glory. His recovery and return to management **symbolised hope for a club and community** in mourning.

He became a pillar of strength for the survivors, the families of those lost, and the entire Manchester community. He attended funerals, visited hospitals, and provided emotional support. His leadership was **characterised by compassion, determination, and an unwavering commitment to the club's future.**

The rebuilding process was arduous, but Busby's vision never wavered. He carefully blended new talents with the surviving players, creating a team that would go on to achieve remarkable success. The pinnacle came in 1968 when Manchester United won the European Cup, a dream that had been cruelly interrupted a decade earlier. This victory was not just a sporting achievement; it was a poignant tribute to those lost in Munich and a testament to the indomitable spirit of Busby and his team.

His story remains an inspiring example of resilience in the face of tragedy and the power of sport to heal and unite.

BOXING THE BOX

Honouring my Purpose: Training for a Sanctioned Bout

Entering the ring in a sanctioned fight became a personal goal, with Addison's disease presenting a formidable challenge. However, with the support of coaches and crew and adapting my approach, **I was determined to break through this roadblock.**

In early 2021, I began regular training sessions with my boxing coach, Jamie Riley, at his gym, Fit Fighters, in Bondi Junction. The gym's atmosphere was electric, embodying the essence of boxing. Red bags swayed like branches in the wind, with the sound of motivated clients punching them in various combinations. The black-tiled floor provided the perfect space for foot drills, refining defence and attack moves. Jamie's use of noodles for slip practice and the satisfying sound of landing jabs on boxing pads created an immersive training experience.

Jamie was more than just a coach; he was my mentor, confidant, and guide. He was always in my corner, whether training in his gym or adapting to park sessions due to COVID guidelines.

Jamie understood me deeply and consistently brought out my best.

The supportive crew

I also committed to a three-month boxing program at a city gym, culminating in a fight night at a stunning venue. The coaches were aware of my Addison's disease and tailored the training accordingly, **providing support when needed and pushing me when appropriate.** My fellow trainees were incredibly supportive, understanding the vision behind WGBC and even helping to raise funds for the cause.

During Pride Month in June, many coaches and crew members recorded videos and pictures with the message **"Boxing is for everyone,"** demonstrating their allyship and support. When Sydney went into lockdown due to COVID-19, the gym showed remarkable commitment by restarting the entire twelve-week program at no additional cost once restrictions were lifted.

This training and preparation period was about physical conditioning and reinforcing my commitment to the values of inclusivity and perseverance that WGBC represents. Every training session and every moment of support from my boxing community **strengthened my resolve to make a difference in the sport and society.**

I want to thank everyone who supported and helped with the fundraising.

Support from the Governing bodies and Global Media

I appreciated the support received from major boxing organisations. It helped to bolster the purpose. The **IBO, WBO, WBA, and WBC** all provided statements of support, with the WBC going above and beyond. They appointed an ambassador and provided letters and video messages of support. They even arranged encouraging messages from world champion boxers and the **legendary Gleason's gym, where Muhammad Ali trained.**

The growing momentum and global coverage.

This support, combined with regular content shared on social media, led to increased visibility through podcast interviews and speaking engagements at virtual events. It attracted worldwide media coverage, including features in LGBTQ+ magazines and mainstream media.

A turning point came when I read an article on CNN. I contacted the journalist, pitching my story and highlighting the support from Boxing Australia, Boxing NSW, and other organisations. I shared my training experience, the reason for creating WGBC, and my journey of overcoming Addison's disease.

Months later, CNN published a thought-provoking, well-written article capturing my vision and mission. The story featured a photo of me in Stark tartan, proudly representing my heritage in a headline article of the world's leading news organisation. This exposure **provided a game-changing opportunity to share WGBC's vital message.**

The CNN article caught the attention of SBS News, an Australian television channel. They invited me for an interview at Jamie's gym in Bondi Junction. My keynote speaking experience proved invaluable during the recording. Jamie also gave a fantastic interview, noting my hard work.

This media coverage amplified WGBC's message and **validated the importance of our mission.** It demonstrated that boxing was alive and thriving, especially at the grassroots level. **It highlighted a growing recognition of the need for inclusion in the sport.**

Integrity and Doing What's Right – DEI Forum and Trans Policy

The challenges of 2021 led to unexpected connections and friendships based on shared values. Every Monday, I joined like-minded, purpose-driven individuals on Zoom, supporting each other through lockdown difficulties. We shared stories and fostered a sense of belonging through our passion for meaningful diversity, equity, and inclusion.

We organised monthly DEI virtual forums featuring speakers worldwide sharing their stories with global audiences. **These powerful storytelling sessions educated and inspired**, leading to think-tank discussions on implementing what we had learned. The eventual in-person meetings with these new friends, eager to watch my upcoming boxing fight, **were a testament to the strong bonds formed during this challenging time.**

The framework that prioritises Safety and Wellbeing

On 17 November 2021, the IOC released its Framework on Fairness, Inclusion and Non-discrimination based on gender identity and sex variations.[22]

It acknowledged eligibility criteria have a crucial role in ensuring safety and fairness in highly organised sports, specifically in the women's category.

The Framework guides organisations to develop trans-inclusive policies applicable to their sport rather than a blanket approach based on testosterone. The safety, health and wellbeing of all athletes is of paramount importance.

It stipulates that policies should consider ten principles, including:

- **Section 4 Fairness:** *No athletes should have an unfair advantage. This includes preventing risks to the physical safety of others and preventing athletes from falsely claiming a gender identity.*

- **Section 6 Evidence-Based Approach:** *Eligibility criteria should be based on robust and peer-reviewed research that prioritises the physical safety of other athletes, no unfair advantage, unpreventable risks.*

- **Section 8: Stakeholder-Centred Approach:** *To prevent harm, organisations should consult with a cross-section of athletes who may be negatively affected.*

---

22 https://stillmed.olympics.com/media/Documents/Beyond-the-Games/Human-Rights/IOC-Framework-Fairness-Inclusion-Non-discrimination-2021.pdf

Leadership and community engagement during winds of rhetoric.

The rhetoric against trans and nonbinary individuals in sports has sparked animosity and intolerance. Armchair critics not previously invested in women's sports suddenly positioned themselves as strong equality proponents. **This process demonised vulnerable individuals.** Around one-millionth of a percent of the world's population will ever participate in the Olympic Games. Sport is better when athletes participate meaningfully and safely with dignity, integrity, and respect.

Inclusion for some should not lead to the exclusion of many or the regression of hard-earned progress.

The wisest approach is to make difficult decisions based on science, **consult relevant parties, ensure fairness, and prioritise safety.** It would have been better if the critics had read the IOC guidelines. They could have encouraged sports organisations to follow them, conduct research relevant to their sport, and consult all affected athletes. Ideally, sufficient funding would be provided for this essential work, ongoing research, and consultation, with regular reviews and engagement of all affected parties.

A specialist LGBTQ+ sporting organisation conducted a community consultation, gathering the views of trans boxers, cisgender boxers, and boxing experts. They also reviewed trans-boxing policies and conducted research. **This work was groundbreaking.** It's important to clarify that the policy was explicitly for WGBC's boxing event.

The policy was shared with all participants well in advance of the event.

WHAT CAN WE LEARN FROM THE OCEAN'S COMMUNICATORS?

The friendly pod

Dolphins, nature's acrobats of the sea, are marvels of social intelligence and cooperation. These sleek, playful mammals live in tight-knit pods, demonstrating unwavering commitment to their family units. When faced with predators like sharks, dolphins employ **sophisticated defensive strategies, forming protective circles around vulnerable members** and using their powerful tails to deliver forceful blows.

Their hunting prowess is equally impressive. Pods perfectly synchronise to herd fish into bait balls or drive them onto shorelines, showcasing their **remarkable teamwork and communication skills**.

Dolphins' interactions with humans reveal their curiosity and intelligence. They often approach divers and swimmers **with playful enthusiasm**. Their ability to understand and respond to human gestures and vocalisations demonstrates a unique form of inter-species communication. Swimming alongside these magnificent creatures can be **a transformative experience**, offering insights into their **world of harmony and social cohesion**.

The Science Times published an excellent article in July 2020 about three ways humans can learn from dolphins:

- *Spend more time with close friends.*
- *It's okay to have preferences in your inner circle. These relationships should be based on trust and loyalty.*
- *A successful career involves strategic networking and building healthy professional relationships, skills we usually develop during adulthood.*[23]

How can you Learn from Dolphins?

Dolphins, the **ocean's powerful communicators,** offer many lessons for those willing to dive deep into their world. These intelligent marine mammals **inspire us with their social bonds, adaptability, and joyful approach to life.** By observing these aquatic wonders, you can gain valuable insights.

---

[23] Hannah C. "3 Lessons We Can Learn From Dolphins" (Science Times Jul 24, 2020) https://www.sciencetimes.com/articles/26601/20200724/3-lessons-learn-dolphins.htm

Here are six ways you can learn from dolphins:

1. **Emotional Intelligence:** Dolphins' ability to read and respond to the emotions of their pod members and even humans teaches the importance of empathy and emotional awareness in our interactions.
2. **Playfulness in Problem-Solving:** Their playful approach to challenges reminds us that creativity and a positive attitude can lead to innovative solutions in our own lives.
3. **Nonverbal Communication:** Dolphins' use of body language and vocalisations emphasises the power of nonverbal cues to enhance our communication skills.
4. **Collaborative Effort:** Their coordinated hunting techniques showcase the effectiveness of teamwork and how collective effort can achieve goals that seem impossible individually.
5. **Adaptability to Environment:** Dolphins' ability to thrive in various marine ecosystems demonstrates the importance of flexibility and adaptability in changing circumstances.
6. **Trust-Building:** Dolphins' interactions with humans in the wild highlight the value of building trust through consistent, positive interactions, even across different species or cultures.

COURAGE IN ACTION

The brave souls who fought for rights during the first Mardi Gras in 1978 did what was right. It was not easy. At that time, male homosexuality was illegal, and there was widespread discrimination and prejudice against the LGBTQ+ community.

They took incredible risks and had the utmost courage to openly express their identity, even though they knew the consequences would be severe.

They risked facing violence, prosecution, rejection from friends and family, and potentially losing their homes and jobs. The 1978 participants

Committing to Your Values

followed the example set a decade earlier in the Stonewall Riots in New York. **They were courageous trailblazers.**

These pioneers understood that progress often comes at a tremendous personal cost. They knew that the path to equality and acceptance would be **long and arduous, but they chose to take those first crucial steps**. Their actions were not just about personal expression; they laid the groundwork for future generations to live more freely and authentically.

The 1969 Stonewall Riots in New York City catalysed the global LGBTQ+ rights movement. When police raided the Stonewall Inn, patrons fought back, sparking days of protests. This watershed moment demonstrated the power of standing together. The ripples from Stonewall reached Australian shores, inspiring local activists **take similar bold actions.**

In the decades since that first Mardi Gras, Australia has seen significant progress in LGBTQ+ rights, but each step forward has **required unwavering commitment to values** of equality and justice. The journey to marriage equality in Australia is a prime example. Despite widespread public support, it took years of campaigning, lobbying, and personal storytelling before same-sex marriage was finally legalised in 2017.

The postal survey on marriage equality was considerably tough for many in the LGBTQ+ community. It exposed us to public debate about our personal lives and relationships. Yet **equality supporters engaged in respectful dialogue,** shared their stories, and campaigned tirelessly. We did what was right, not easy, by advocating for full rights in the face of opposition and sometimes hurtful rhetoric.

Courageous people consistently choose the path of integrity over convenience.

Exercise: Mentoring with Whiskers – The Grumpy Cat's Challenge

OBJECTIVE: *Developing empathy and courage to do what's right, even when uncomfortable*

COURAGE

This exercise aims to help you strengthen your moral fibre by:

1. Recognising the importance of mentoring, even when it's outside your comfort zone.
2. Understanding the value of second chances and personal growth.
3. Acknowledging the difficulty of overcoming your nature for the greater good.
4. Experiencing the satisfaction of helping others improve.
5. Learning to support others despite personal discomfort.
6. Reflecting on personal growth and increased empathy after facing challenges.

This exercise assists in developing courage, empathy, problem-solving skills, and emotional intelligence.

Imaginary Scene

You're Humphrey, the famously grumpy cat at the Bytes & Whiskers Data Centre. You've always ruled the roost with your YouTube following and notorious "Humphrey special" scratches. Your typical day involves napping on server racks, chasing cursor icons across monitors, and occasionally causing network outages with a well-placed paw.

Enter Tiddles, a fresh-faced feline straight out of Cat College. In his eagerness to impress by being the team joker, Tiddles has been bringing live brown snakes into the data centre through the cat flap. Brown snakes are the second most venomous land snakes in the world. The human staff is terrified, and there's talk of having Tiddles transferred.

Your owner sits you down for a chat. "Humphrey," they say, scratching behind your ears, "I know you'd rather nap on the warm servers than deal with this, but Tiddles needs your help. Remember when you first started and accidentally unplugged the entire eastern seaboard? We all make mistakes."

Committing to Your Values

You look at your owner skeptically, wondering if this conversation is worth missing your main nap of the day for.

"You need to chat with him," they continue, ignoring your grumpy meow of protest. "Get him to apologise, show him the ropes. And try to get the team to calm down. Think of it as… a unique training opportunity?"

Your expression clearly says, "I'd rather eat a hairball," but your owner presses on. "Who knows? Maybe Tiddles can be our official… uh… reptile detection system?"

With a sigh that could wilt flowers, you reluctantly agree. You can almost hear yourself thinking, "The things I do for treats."

Reflection Questions

1. How did you feel about mentoring Tiddles despite your grumpy nature?
2. What role does your experience play in your ability to help Tiddles?
3. How might this experience change your approach to future challenges, and what lessons can you draw from it to help others overcome their mistakes?

For each of the six pillars of courage, identify a personal memory related to mentoring someone or helping them overcome a mistake, especially when it was outside their comfort zone. Reflect on how these memories can help you face future challenges and be a role model for others, much like Humphrey needs to be for Tiddles.

Scenario 1: Helping a Colleague Adapt to New Technology (Example)

Emotional Courage Memory: Sharing personal struggles and frustrations when learning the new system, creating a safe space for a colleague to express their concerns.

COURAGE

Physical Courage Memory: Staying late after work for a week to help the colleague practice using the new software, despite a preference for maintaining a strict work-life balance.

Moral Courage Memory: Speaking up in a team meeting when others mocked the colleague's slow progress, emphasising the importance of patience and support during transitions.

Empathetic Courage Memory: Understanding the colleague's specific challenges with the new technology and adjusting the teaching approach to match their learning style.

Steadfast Courage Memory: Committed to weekly check-ins with the colleague for three months, offering consistent support even when the personal workload was heavy.

Cerebral Courage Memory: Developing a simplified user guide for the new system, incorporating visual aids and step-by-step instructions, which was later adopted by the entire department.

Scenario 2: Helping a Friend Overcome a Fear (Your Turn)

Think about when you needed to help a friend face a fear. Use the Courage Bank concept to identify memories that can help you be a supportive and courageous friend. Fill in your memories for each type of courage:

Emotional Courage: The willingness to open up to a broad spectrum of emotions.

Memory:

Physical Courage: Acting bravely in the face of fear or pain.

Memory:

Committing to Your Values

Moral Courage: Taking a firm stand for your beliefs and committing to your values.

Memory:

Empathetic Courage: Understanding others, practising humility, and setting aside personal bias.

Memory:

Steadfast Courage: Being resolute, focused, and purposeful.

Memory:

Cerebral Courage: Disruption, innovation, and driving change.

Memory:

Remember to approach these questions with honesty and self-compassion. Your development journey is unique, and every step forward, no matter how small, is progress.

WRAP UP

Committing to your values is about staying true to what you believe in. It is tough, but others see you as a person of impeccable trust. It involves epitomising ethical behaviour, leading by example, and inspiring others to do the right thing.

COURAGE

Consistently **choosing integrity over convenience** and staying committed to your values makes **you stride through hurdles with purpose.** It creates space for personal and team growth. Your values are not constraints but guides pointing **towards areas of development and impact.**

Use them as your anchors, propelling you to success and delivering positive change.

My three key learnings:

1. Sir Matt Busby's rebuilding Manchester United after the Munich air disaster shows how values can transform tragedy into triumph and help communities.

2. Training for a sanctioned boxing competition demonstrated my commitment to my purpose.

3. Dolphins are cool! They are excellent communicators.

What are your three learnings?

CHAPTER TEN

NORMALISE COURAGE

CHAPTER TEN
Make Courage the Norm

WHO HELPED YOU FLOURISH AND GROW?

Great teachers have an uncanny ability to see potential in their students that often remains hidden. They're like skilled gardeners, nurturing dormant seeds of talent and character, waiting for the right conditions to sprout and bloom. These educators don't just impart knowledge; they cultivate life stories, meeting each student where they are and guiding them towards where they could be.

Consider that teacher who saw your unique strengths, even when you did not fully appreciate your capabilities. Perhaps a high school teacher saw a budding writer in a shy student struggling with self-expression. They gently encouraged you to share your thoughts on paper, allowing your voice to emerge and grow stronger.

Lawrence R. Samuel Ph.D. explained how teachers are a central figure in our lives in his article May 2024 article, highlighting:

- *Teachers can have a profound, positive impact on a young person's life.*
- *People tend to undervalue teachers' role in shaping students' minds.*
- *People's personalities as adults can have much to do with the direction a teacher provides.*[24]

When life's ups and downs threatened to derail your progress, they were there, offering not just academic guidance but also emotional fortitude. They taught travelling through life not through lectures but by example,

---

[24] Lawrence R. Samuel Ph.D. "How Teachers Change Lives" (Psychology Today May 22, 2024) https://www.psychologytoday.com/intl/blog/psychology-yesterday/202405/how-teachers-change-lives

showing you how to face adversity with grace and determination. Their unwavering belief in you filled your spirit with self-belief and confidence. They left an indelible imprint of courage on your heart and mind. When faced with inevitable obstacles, you might ask, "What would they say?".

Their wisdom and encouragement became a guiding light, illuminating paths through darkness and uncertainty.

WHAT IS MAKING COURAGE THE NORM?

We make courage the norm by accepting where others are and acknowledging their mistakes. **There are various roads to bravery.** Some might already be on the freeway, a few might be leaving the car park, and others might ask a friendly face for directions after taking a wrong turn. I accepted where I was in my boxing journey by learning from each misstep. An early mistake probably resulted in a literal punch in the face! I discovered how to adapt. **A coach in my corner supported and encouraged me to keep pushing forward.**

When you are the coach in the individual or team's corner, **you guide them with a hand-up** instead of making it easy, and **you avoid missing crucial learning with a hand-out.**

In this nurturing space, you provide a "bravery mirror" and a "fright forcefield." The bravery mirror reflects the potential within each individual, showing them the grit they possess but might not yet grasp. It's a tool **that helps them see their strength**, capacity for growth, and ability to overcome.

On the other hand, the fright forcefield acts as a protective barrier. It allows others to draw inspiration and courage from your example without being overwhelmed by their frights and doubts. **It's not about shielding them from obstacles but rather from the chilling effects of self-doubt and excessive fear.** This approach empowers individuals to find their inner strength and keep adapting and moving forward, regardless of setbacks. It's about **creating a culture where courage is admired and becomes as natural as breathing.**

By fostering this environment, you help others scrape the magic dust off their courage without reabsorbing their fear. You guide them to discover courage, which isn't the **absence of fear but the determination to advance despite it.**

You show them that every step, no matter how small, is a victory on the path to bravery.

Josephine Baker's Example

Josephine Baker, born in 1906 in St. Louis, Missouri, embodied tremendous courage and bravery throughout her extraordinary life. **She served as a powerful role model** for generations. Despite growing up in poverty and confronting racial discrimination, **she fearlessly defied societal constraints and pursued her aspirations.** Her bold move to Paris in 1925 defied racial barriers and allowed her to thrive in a world that fully appreciated her talent and charisma.

In Paris, Josephine Baker's fearless performances at the Folies Bergère showcased her audacity and skill. She defied conventional notions of modesty and racial stereotypes, using her art as a powerful self-expression and social commentary. **She supported Panama Al Brown.**

Baker's courage extended far beyond the stage. During World War II, she demonstrated extraordinary bravery as an intelligence agent for the French Resistance. She used her celebrity status to gather crucial information on German officials at high-society events.

Baker's **commitment to civil rights further cemented her status as a paragon of courage**. Returning to the United States in the 1950s, she boldly refused to perform for segregated audiences, insisting on integrated shows. This stance challenged the status quo and helped desegregate many venues nationwide. **In 1963, she stood alongside Martin Luther King Jr., the only official female speaker at the March on Washington, using her platform to advocate for equality and justice.**

Her deliberate choice to adopt twelve children from different countries, forming her "Rainbow Tribe," unequivocally affirmed her belief in the

COURAGE

supremacy of love and understanding to surpass racial and cultural barriers. This multicultural family **undeniably epitomised her values, unequivocally showcasing the potential for harmony and unity within diversity.**

Fearlessly pursuing her dreams, standing up for her beliefs, and showing compassion to others, she symbolised courage for those around her. She emphasised the importance of fostering understanding and **showing respect in our relationships with others, ultimately contributing to a fairer and more inclusive world.**

Her legacy serves as a poignant reminder that courage extends beyond individual acts of bravery.

COURAGE IN THE RING AND BEYOND
Bravery in Action

A yellow mohawk and the gayest 1980s track as my walkout song.

Fight week preparation involved a couple of technique classes, discovering my opponent and a four-hour hair appointment. The man I was fighting was a good friend. Alex Whitlock is a gentleman. The company organising the bout contacted him and asked if he would fight me. The matchmakers ensured a fair and safe fight based on age, weight, and experience. **Alex is a staunch ally and always encouraged me during training.** I could not have asked for anyone better to celebrate my first fight and demonstrate the values of boxing. We were not fighting each other.

We were mates fighting for a cause and punching through barriers.

The authentic Stark.

Some professional boxers have a penchant for peacocking. A tendency to impress with flashy boxing attire and outrageous behaviour. They show how to make an entrance by making an entrance. They deserve this after all the **arduous training and intense preparation.** It brings glitz, flamboyant glamour, and Oscar-worthy entertainment. The crowd love it!

Make Courage the Norm

A gay boxer who is the boss of a gay boxing organisation needed to bring a Stark spark.

The fight uniform was black shorts with a white top. The company arranged for the WGBC logo to be printed on the back. Cut, bleach, tone, and style my fashionable mohawk took four hours. Hair spray deterred any canaries from mistaking my locks for a flock to hang out with. Alex and I had the first match of the evening. Moments before walking out, we made a pact to touch gloves at the beginning of every round. **This is a tradition and mark of respect when sparring,** but it is not usually done in a fight.

Harnessing 1980s bravery.

My walkout song was Relax by Frankie Goes to Hollywood, the 1980s chart-topping gay anthem whose video was banned from television for being too gay. **The thunderous rhythmic beats signalled my entrance**, having proudly adorned my body with a rainbow flag. There was a diva moment walking back, putting my arm around the boxing coach accompanying me into the ring. My sturdy mohawk stood upright when he put the head guard on me.

Alex received a rapturous welcome, and I was thrilled when he entered the ring. We touched gloves when the bell dinged at the start of the round. I had taken extra doses of hydrocortisone. The intense six minutes of fighting physicality would stretch me to the max. We landed good shots with lots of combos. Big Ben's younger brother chimed a welcoming 60-second reprieve. **I listened to the coach, whom I trusted implicitly.** A swig of water and up again touching Alex's glove at the start of round two.

I was a bit lacklustre until my coach shouted, *"Martin right hook!" It's my best boxing move and purpose. Fighting homophobia hooked me to fight for what is right: equality and fairness.* My right hook landed on Alex's temple once, twice and a few more times. It was my best round of the fight. The dings came at the right time. It was tiring! The one-minute break felt like 10 seconds.

COURAGE

The courage corner.

I did my best in round three, with both landing our combos. I was flagging. Alex's coach supported Alex, but he uttered six words of encouragement: **"Martin, there's 50 seconds; keep going!"** He knew I just needed to get through to the end. Phew, the final dings.

I didn't care about winning or losing. We both won the vital fight.

I congratulated Alex on his win.

My husband, WGBC Board, friends from the DEI forum and other close friends were there to support me. Their voices sounded like they had all done 12 rounds with Anthony Joshua. There were hugs, smiles and lots of tears. I went upstairs and found an empty room called Jenny, who was in Singapore and cried. **Jenny listened and understood.** The rest of the evening, I was cheering on the other boxers and spending time with everyone there supporting me.

My family in the UK watched the fight live on Facebook. I have seen nervous parents watching their adult children fight in a boxing match. **Mums don't always shake the habit of grabbing an arm at the first sign of danger.** There was a 16,000km distance between Mum's swift and nifty wrists and my boxing gloves. Thankfully, I was just out of reach – only 0.5km in it!

Thank you to everyone who helped organise the night and supported me. A big thank you to Alex and the other boxers who raised money for WGBC and causes they cared about.

RECOGNITION AND GRAPPLING WITH DEPRESSION

February 2022 brought good news: a message from a LinkedIn News Editor. After thousands of hours on the platform, this was the first message from LinkedIn News. I had consistently posted quality content

Make Courage the Norm

with a simple, coherent message of courage and inclusion. Opening the message was like eating a slice of Nan's delicious apple and blackberry pie; it was great news. I was to be included in LinkedIn's inaugural Top LGBTQIA+ Voices list.

LinkedIn's Top Voices program **recognises influential experts across various professional fields.** The blue LinkedIn Top Voice badge is invitation-only and signifies a prestigious honour. How exciting to be joining the ranks of Barack Obama, Brené Brown, Simon Sinek, Melinda Gates, and Snoop Dogg, all Top Voices. When the list was published, I received lovely congratulatory messages from my LinkedIn family in Australia and worldwide.

The return of an unwelcome companion.

In May 2022, depression returned. I was more sensitive to situations, my mood darkened, enjoying things less and little focus on things to look forward to. As the depression progressed, the symptoms worsened. It was debilitating. The enormity of organising the Championships and the angrier, less tolerant, hyperconnected 2020s world compounded made it worse. **I sought help early by seeing my excellent GP,** who prescribed antidepressants and arranged a mental health plan. **Staying away from triggers and sharing with people I knew, liked, and trusted helped immensely.** Some days, I withdrew and fell into a cocoon. Some obnoxious social commentators dismiss sensitivity as lily-livered weaklings living in igloos built from blizzards of snowflakes.

A single ice crystal joins others to form a beautiful snowfall shaped by its experience of moving through the atmosphere and falling through different zones and temperatures. If snowflakes were sentient, would they choose to land in our human world or decide to break up in the atmosphere? Why is cruelty sometimes a response to humans filled with goodness, compassion, and kindness? *I took a four-month break from social media to protect my mental health.* The price of standing up against hatred can be your mental health. Usually, trolling does not bother me, and I would not even look at their keyboard toxicity. I did not want to allow them to cause me harm.

Two great techniques from boxing serve as self-defence for our mental health in social media: stepping away and blocking. Blocking stops the bully in their tracks. Stepping away keeps the bully in their echo chamber of hate.

When the only voice they hear is a poisonous diatribe, they might discover their ears need an antidote of dignity, courtesy, and respect.

Support systems and Boundaries

After struggling with depression for over four decades, there have been many conversations with individuals who have also dealt with this condition. I have listened to psychologists and mental health experts at events, on podcasts, and on television. I've observed three common traits among those who claim to be supportive of people with depression but often end up doing the opposite:

1. Selfish indifference: People who don't care and may criticise or humiliate you.
2. The "I'm OK, and so should you be" brigade: Those who dismiss your concerns and use gaslighting.
3. Performative support: Offering sympathy without meaningful action or changes.

I am fortunate to have a fantastic husband, family, and close friends who were there for me during tough and not-so-good times when things weren't great. Their presence made a significant difference. They listened and cared for me. It helped immensely. **There was a supportive network of people who genuinely cared.** They checked in with me, listened when I burst into tears, went for walks, and caught up for coffee. Some even hit the pads and boxing bags with me.

They were there, knowing I would get through this challenging and painful time.

One situation made it worse. Imagine encountering someone who seems outwardly caring and compassionate, and your empathy draws them to you. Your kind brightness attracts their energy-zapping fervency. It's like having days – of butterflies hovering around you and nights – of moths not leaving when you turn off the lights. The following day, you wake up to find moth skins everywhere. You see caterpillars crawling towards you.

They want you to be their protective shell.

They metamorphose into winged creatures, exiting a self-making crisis chrysalis. This person takes advantage of your kindness, bombarding you with messages, texts, voicemails, and social media communications, refusing to leave you alone even after you ask them to stop. You block them, but they still find ways to contact you. The only way to stop them is to report them to the police.

We live in an era where people can contact you any time, any place, anywhere. They can reach you through various means, such as sending excessive messages and voicemails. When you tell them to stop, they may not change. **Do not be afraid to act and report such behaviour to the authorities.**

Your happiness, mental health, and well-being are paramount.

WHAT CAN WE LEARN FROM NATURE'S BOXERS?

The Bouncing Champions

Red kangaroos, nature's heavyweight champions, are the genuine boxers of the animal kingdom. These muscular marsupials, with their powerful hind legs and robust tails, are not just built for agility and combat but also for resilience. In the unforgiving Australian outback, **they face epic challenges, yet they persist.**

Kangaroos' playful nature and community spirit offer valuable lessons in resilience. Their social structure, known as a mob, demonstrates the

COURAGE

power of the community in facing challenges. Their ability to communicate through body language and vocalisations highlights the **importance of clear, non-verbal communication in group dynamics.** Combined with their tenacity, these traits make kangaroos true champions of the Australian outback.

During droughts, when the land turns to dust and water becomes scarce, red kangaroos showcase their extraordinary survival skills. They can go for long periods without drinking, extracting moisture from the vegetation they consume. Their ability to modify their diet to whatever sparse foliage is available is a **testament to their adaptability.** This is a necessary trait in tough and harsh times.

When it comes to evading predators, kangaroos are masters of evasion. Their powerful legs allow them to bound up to 56 km/h, covering 8 metres in a single leap. This incredible mobility, agility combined with their keen senses, helps them stay one hop ahead of danger.

Kangaroo mothers face a unique challenge when it's time to wean their joeys. As the young kangaroo grows, it becomes increasingly difficult for the mother to hop with the added weight. Nature's solution? The pouch muscles gradually weaken, making it harder for the joey to stay inside. **This gentle encouragement and the mother's guidance help the young kangaroo transition to independence.**

The University of Sydney shared a fascinating story in December 2020 titled "What's up Skip? Kangaroos really can 'talk' to us" it mentioned kangaroos:

- *can intentionally communicate with humans*
- *gaze at people when problem-solving*
- *are social animals and may be able to adapt their usual social behaviours to interact with humans.*[25]

---

[25] https://www.sydney.edu.au/news-opinion/news/2020/12/16/whats-up-skip-kangaroos-really-can-talk-to-us.html

How can you learn from Kangaroos?

Kangaroos, nature's resilient boxers, offer valuable bravery, adaptability, and community spirit lessons. Even in harsh environments, their playful nature reminds us of the importance of maintaining a positive outlook. The journey of Joey leaving the pouch exemplifies the courage needed to face new challenges. Here are six ways teams can learn from kangaroos:

1. **Fostering Resilience:** Like kangaroos thriving in drought, encourage team members to adapt to challenging situations, viewing obstacles as opportunities for growth.

2. **Promoting Agility:** Emulate the kangaroo's ability to change direction quickly by fostering a culture that embraces change and responds swiftly to new challenges. This strategic agility will make team leaders feel proactive and in control.

3. **Nurturing Gradual Independence:** Mimic the kangaroo's weaning process by gradually increasing team members' responsibilities, allowing them to build confidence over time. This trust in their abilities will make team members feel respected and valued.

4. **Encouraging Playfulness:** Incorporate the kangaroo's playful spirit into your team culture, fostering creativity and reducing fear of failure.

5. **Building Community Spirit:** Like kangaroos in a mob, create a supportive team environment where members look out for each other and face challenges together.

6. **Embracing Leaps of Faith:** Inspire team members to take calculated risks, much like a kangaroo's powerful leap, by creating a safe environment where trying new things is valued and supported.

COURAGE IN ACTION

The aftermath of Cyclone Tracy in Darwin in 1974 is a testament to the courage and resilience of the Australian spirit. In the face of utter devastation, the community rallied to rebuild their city and their collective hope and determination.

COURAGE

They took incredible risks and showed utmost courage to return and rebuild, even though they knew the challenges would be immense. The destruction was almost complete, with over 70% of Darwin's buildings destroyed or severely damaged. Despite this, the residents of Darwin chose to remain and fight for the future of their city.

These understood that progress often comes at a tremendous personal cost. They knew the path to recovery would be long and arduous, but they took those **crucial steps.** Their actions were not just about rebuilding structures; they laid the groundwork for a stronger, more resilient Darwin.

The rebuilding effort became a catalyst for change in Australian building practices. Engineers and architects **took similar bold actions,** developing new standards for cyclone-resistant construction. Houses were built more robustly, with reinforced frames and specially designed roofs to withstand cyclonic winds. This innovative approach demonstrated the power of turning adversity into progress.

Since Cyclone Tracy, Darwin has seen significant urban planning and disaster preparedness advancements. However, each step forward has **required an unwavering commitment** to safety and community resilience. The journey to creating a cyclone-proof city is a prime example. It took years of research, implementation, and community education to transform Darwin into one of the most cyclone-prepared cities in the world.

The rebuilding process was laborious for many in the community. It exposed them to physical hardships, emotional trauma, and financial strain. Yet **Darwin's residents engaged in supportive dialogue,** shared their experiences, and worked tirelessly to recreate their homes.

They committed to their city's rebirth in the face of overwhelming odds.

Exercise: Boundary Setting – the supportive CEO's challenge

OBJECTIVE: *Develop healthy boundaries and positive support while managing negativity*

Make Courage the Norm

This exercise aims to help you strengthen your interpersonal skills by:

1. Recognising the importance of supporting others, even when challenging.
2. Understanding the value of maintaining boundaries for personal and others' well-being.
3. Acknowledging the difficulty of balancing support and self-care.
4. Experiencing the satisfaction of helping others achieve their goals.
5. Learning to guide others through fear without absorbing their anxiety.
6. Reflecting on personal growth and increased empathy after facing interpersonal challenges.

This exercise assists in developing empathy, problem-solving skills, and emotional intelligence.

Imaginary Scene

You're Doris, the CEO of Croc Bank, and you've arranged to sponsor your friend's first boxing match. It's a fundraiser to support local communities. Your husband Bert has brought all his mates from the pub along. They're raucous and cheering on your friend and the other boxers.

Your friend's relative is nervous and wants their mate to pull out. The relative is about to send your friend a text saying they should withdraw. You understand how much this match means to your friend and how nervous he is.

You approach the relative, knowing you need to guide them through their fear so they can enjoy the moment and support your friend when he needs it the most. You're aware that you need to maintain your boundaries while helping the relative manage their anxiety.

"I know you're worried," you say to the relative. You offer reassurance, "But think about how much this means to your mate. He's trained hard for this and needs our support now more than ever."

COURAGE

The relative looks at you, conflicted. "But what if he gets hurt? I can't bear to watch that."

You take a deep breath, reminding yourself not to absorb their anxiety. "I understand your concern. Boxing has risks, but the organisers have taken every precaution.

Your mate is well-prepared, and having your support will mean the world to him. Let's focus on cheering him on instead of worrying about what might happen."

Your mate wins the fight. You ask the relative. "Why were you scared?" The response turns into a conversation focusing on the relative working through their fears.

Reflection Questions

1. How did you feel about guiding the relative through their fear?
2. What role does your experience play in your ability to help manage this situation?
3. How might this change your approach to future challenges, and what lessons can you draw from it to help others overcome their fears without compromising your well-being?

For each of the six pillars of courage, identify a personal memory related to supporting someone while maintaining healthy boundaries, especially when it was outside your comfort zone. Reflect on how these memories can help you face future challenges and be a role model for others, much like Doris needs to be for the relative.

Scenario 1: Helping a Colleague Adapt to New Framework (Example)

Emotional Courage Memory: Holding an open discussion and feedback session where the colleague can freely express their fears and frustrations with the new framework.

Physical Courage Memory: Offering to demonstrate the new framework's key features in a team meeting, taking the pressure off the struggling colleague and motivating them to practise more.

Moral Courage Memory: Advocating for realistic deadlines for framework proficiency in team meetings, supporting the colleague without singling them out or oversharing their struggles.

Empathetic Courage Memory: Recognising the colleague's learning style differed from the standard training approach and suggesting alternative resources that might better suit their needs without taking on the role of their tutor.

Steadfast Courage Memory: Setting up a recurring 30-minute weekly or fortnightly informal check-in with the colleague to discuss framework progress.

Cerebral Courage Memory: Developing a concise 'cheat sheet' for the most commonly used framework features, helping the colleague gain confidence quickly while encouraging them to expand their knowledge independently.

Scenario 2: Helping a Friend Overcome a Fear (Your Turn)

Think about when you needed to help a friend face a fear. Use the Courage Bank concept to identify memories that can help you be a supportive and courageous friend. Fill in your memories for each type of courage:

Emotional Courage: The willingness to open up to a broad spectrum of emotions.

Memory:

Physical Courage: Acting bravely in the face of fear or pain.

Memory:

COURAGE

Moral Courage: Taking a firm stand for what you believe in and committing to your values.

Memory:

Empathetic Courage: Understanding others, practising humility, and setting aside personal bias.

Memory:

Steadfast Courage: Being resolute, focused, and purposeful.

Memory:

Cerebral Courage: Disruption, innovation, and driving change.

Memory:

Remember to approach these questions with honesty and self-compassion. Your development journey is unique, and every step forward, no matter how small, is progress.

WRAP UP

You make courage the norm by accepting where others are in their journey to bravery. Reinforcement of courageous behaviour with positive language boosts confidence and resilience.

Just as in boxing, where a coach in your corner provides guidance and support, you can be that coach for others in life. By offering a "bravery

Make Courage the Norm

mirror" and a "fright forcefield," you enable others to tap into their courage without fear.

You transfer privilege by lifting others along the way.

My three key learnings:

1. With my bright yellow mohawk and a classic 1980s gay anthem walkout song, I brought courage and made gay boxing the norm.
2. My coach's encouragement and Alex's sportsmanship reminded me that mistakes are part of the journey.
3. I learned from Joeys the wisdom of being pushed out of the pouch.

What are your three learnings?

CHAPTER ELEVEN

BE CONSISTENT

CHAPTER ELEVEN

Be consistent – dont just keep thinking

WHAT IS YOUR INNER SUPERHERO?

Courage breaks through mental barriers, providing the trailblazer with the aptitude and attitude to boldly deliver their vision. Having the courage of your convictions is a formidable and universal superpower that anyone can access. We are all scared from time to time. When fright freezes you, deploying this superpower is a powerful heater. It transforms a cessation into a resumption.

A novice jogger takes a massive stride by joining a running club. Practising week after week and improving their gait opens the doors to half marathons and completing a marathon. Their friends and acquaintances tell stories of seeing the jogger becoming an accomplished marathon runner through determination.

Nauman Naeem M.D. published an article in July 2024 about the rise of superhero culture and why it matters, mentioning:

- *Superheroes have become a major part of popular culture in recent decades.*
- *Their popularity goes beyond entertainment, representing hope in the face of rising global challenges.*
- *We are each responsible for the world we create and must find inner strength to overcome our global problems.*[26]

---

[26] Nauman Naeem M.D. "The Rise of Superhero Culture and Why It Matters" (Psychology Today July 29, 2024 https://www.psychologytoday.com/au/blog/the-universe-within/202407/the-rise-of-superhero-culture-and-why-it-matters

COURAGE

How many people does it take to change a lightbulb? Lightbulbs are changed when you stop thinking and start doing. You might need help from a friend to get the stepladder. They might hold it steady as you climb the steps, enabling the light to shine. By turning ideas into concrete steps, you move from thought to action, transforming plans into reality.

Courage turns mental mountains into molehills, providing the strength to deliver on your vision.

WHAT IS BE CONSISTENT, AND DON'T JUST KEEP THINKING?

Deciding to deliver and getting on with it is often easier than delaying. **Delayflation requires more heavy lifting, extra time and resources, and probably more precious dollars to do what you could have done had you not stopped.** This especially rings true when you have the support of allies and friends. This approach conserves good energy. It channels it into productive outcomes rather than letting it drown through overthinking or hesitation. With the backing of those who believe in you, committing to action leads to sustainable successes and repeatable outcomes.

It ensures your efforts are bolstered through ballast and not blustered away through winds of doubt and complacency.

Delaying action only makes the task harder. Kicking the can down the road is you putting the boot in. Why make things more complicated? With the support of allies and friends, you can find the energy to push through.

Committing to action leads to sustainable successes and meaningful results.

How you show up and who shows up is the core of the community. There will be people on the sidelines cheering you on. **Others will see your cheerleaders, and they will see you.** What you communicate amplifies. What the community communicates becomes the most prominent speaker in the world. That is a collective voice of change echoing in the abundant ocean of the digital age, whether on social media, in the news, or in coffee conversations. This is how you build a courage cascade: **one person with a bold vision, consistently communicating it over the years,** making what has never happened before something that can happen again and again.

Success occurs again much quicker than initially envisaged.

The Allyship Example

Buddy Oldman, a courageous Wiradjuri man, registered for the Championships. The Wiradjuri are the largest Aboriginal group in New South Wales. Buddy participated in a boxing competition in Sydney in October 2022. **I had to go along to support him.**

Before I could enter, a man with a beaming smile, picturesque eyes, and a serene heart ran out to hug me. **The comforting hug had a sturdy shoulder to rest my troubled mind.** The huddle had two hearts beating in unison. Buddy said," What you are doing is amazing, brother. I am here for you. None of the fuckers giving you grief online have 1% of your courage!"

His palpable empathy matched his ropable revulsion for the homophobia and bullying I was experiencing on social media. He shared the wisdom, "It only takes one suicide attempt to be successful." Buddy was the coach in my corner. He offered to be there 24 hours a day, seven days a week.

A champion act of allyship and visible support.

Allyship is not hard, you can do it with EASE:

- **Educate** *yourself by exploring resources, listening to lived experiences, and, most importantly, respecting boundaries. This shows your consideration and empathy. Don't rely on those who have experienced prejudice to educate you; ask questions only if they are comfortable* sharing. It's okay to make mistakes. **Remember, impact matters more than intent.** We all know the **fine line between offensive and misunderstanding.**

- **Amplify** *the messages of others by using your platforms and* **networks to share someone's story without centring yourself.** *This is an act of support and inclusivity. You can transfer your privilege to open doors and* **provide access to spaces and opportunities.**

- **Speak Up** *when you witness or hear discriminatory behaviour.* **Say something or report it,** *but always consider the physical and psychological safety of yourself and others. You can lodge a report in person or online later if you can't speak out due to safety concerns.*

- **Engage** *with other people and communities by inviting and being invited.* **Turn barriers into opportunities to connect and build genuine rapport.** *Respecting healthy boundaries fosters respectful relationships that can grow into friendships.*

WHAT IS BE CONSISTENT, AND DON'T JUST KEEP THINKING?

Taking Ownership and Support

Organising the Championships helped me through my depression. I arranged the insurance, hosts, photographers, DJ, contract for selling the tickets, and camera for live streaming the Championships. There was a series of meetings with the Combat Sports Authority to discuss the transgender policy, briefing them on the safety-first approach. I became a registered boxing promoter. The permit for the Championships stipulated **my accountability to ensure compliance with the trans policy.** Promoters who breach the combat sports laws can be prosecuted and fined tens of thousands of dollars or receive a custodial sentence. **I took responsibility and was prepared to put my financial and personal freedom on the line.**

There is nothing to fear when you do the right thing.

Be consistent – dont just keep thinking

Helen Empson, my sister from another mother, flew in from Adelaide the day before the Championships. She was the project manager for Martin. **Helen gives me a look when I'm in trouble,** which is always followed by a **warm, loving smile and hug. I caused trouble to get smiles and hugs.** When you haven't done something before and learn as you go along, **Helen is the person you want there. Things get done with minimal fuss and maximum warmth and compassion.** I could have fled the country confidently shouting, "Helen is in charge; see you in a fortnight!"

The Big Day Arrives

Depression dampened my dream. It was lingering like a long winter delaying spring. In all honesty, I wanted the whole thing to be over. It was considerably stressful. My job was to make the Championships memorable for the boxers and everyone involved. **This was a ground-breaking day, making sporting history happen. Realising the weight of the responsibility was a difficult moment.**

We were joined by our good friends from Boxing New South Wales, exceptional volunteers, a ringside doctor, and the **best boxing judges and referees in Australia and probably the world.** The boxing ring was set up, my boxing coach Jamie was the DJ, and the WGBC Board welcomed guests and helped out. The boxers and their coaches arrived, completing the final entry checks, weigh-ins and medicals. The boxers started warming up for their fights. The lighting and cameras for the live stream were installed. Jenny was taking care of the social media feed; **she was the online cheerleader and commentator.** The spectators arrived excitedly, taking their seats for a ringside seat to watch sporting history happen.

My dream was taking shape. Depression was told to go away for a few hours.

We had two fabulous drag queen emcees who could win any Ru Paul Drag's All-Stars season. **They exuberantly energised the crowd, bringing**

sparkle, glamour, and laughter. Their vitality of love, kindness, and good old-fashioned entertainment had a powerful magnetism that could attract the North and South Poles to Sydney at the peak of summer, transforming sheets of ice into torrential downpours of rainbows with pots of gold found everywhere. They were perfect! Their performances nearly brought the roof down.

The media, including ABC News, attended. I was in and out of the ring, holding the mic, speaking to the crowd, and getting them on their feet in a fun, non-combative shadowboxing competition. **The standard of boxing was superb. I could not be prouder of the boxers.** They worked incredibly hard, showing their extraordinary skills and boxing prowess round after round. They won belts or medals. A trans man fought a cisgender man, winning a world title. It was a safe and fair fight. **All the effort in developing the trans policy and breaking a barrier was worthwhile.** We had a magical second day of boxing, with the Championships wrapping up on a Sunday afternoon.

On the car ride home, Helen said, "Martin, congratulations. Now, you need to relax and decompress." All the Board and my husband agreed. On the way home, **I heard multiple "Congratulations, you did it, I'm proud of you!"**

A huge thanks to all the boxers, officials, supporters, spectators, and everyone who made the Championships a triumphant success. I wish to acknowledge Tony Whelan's incredible public support. The Championships would not have happened without his expert assistance and tremendous help. I also want to thank **Gabrielle Sproat** for designing the beautiful WGBC logo.

Mardi Gras Parade

Sydney was hosting World Pride, the biggest LGBTQ+ festival in the world, and I helped organise one of the major sporting events during the first weekend. For me, the festival was over as it began, apart from the Mardi Gras Parade. A small group of us marched in the parade. Some friends joined at the last minute, for which I am incredibly thankful. We were featured heavily on the ABC TV livestream due to the success and publicity we received from the Championships. When the cameras were there, I decided to do a bit of shadowboxing. Friends called and messaged me, saying, "I saw you on ABC News."

It was beautiful to know friends cared for and celebrated that special moment with me.

Uploading the Championship highlight videos on social media triggered the trolls. Individuals were complaining about an event that had already taken place. **The 'sensitive' bullies thought it was "woke" or "destroying boxing" and extolled the virtues of cancelling WGBC.** In an era of railing against "cancel culture," "defending freedoms," and condemning virtue signalling, the outrage is perplexing.

I deleted all the nastiness, which was 98% of the comments.

From Boxing to Business and Expanding Horizons

My keynote speaking career flourished, with engagements for Australia's largest bank, Commonwealth Bank, NRMA, and TikTok. LinkedIn also invited me to be the keynote speaker for the **launch of a leadership initiative** for senior marketing professionals. This was supported by starting an audio room on LinkedIn **for weekly discussions about courage.**

I launched a LinkedIn course, drawing from my procurement career experience and knowledge about making an impact and achieving success on LinkedIn. My goal was to **help my customers establish meaningful connections,** boost visibility, and position themselves **as trusted authority and thought leaders.** The course included presentations, videos, transcripts, worldwide research, and eBooks. It took months of research and development and several more months to record and compile all the training materials.

COURAGE

Boxing dreams continued to Grow

Boxing wasn't far from my mind. I spoke regularly with people in Chicago. They wanted to bring a team to the Championships but only learned about it a week before it was held. We talked about having the next WGBC in Chicago.

I had always dreamed of taking WGBC to America. One conversation made things happen.

My contacts in Chicago and I started the planning process immediately.

Media Momentum Builds

My publicist, **Nicki Price,** developed an extensive PR campaign, starting with issuing a press release and attracting regular and sustained media coverage. It began with articles in Chicago and LGBTQ+ publications. The momentum continued to build, with a significant sports publication reporting that WGBC would be held in Chicago.

This article was featured alongside a story about Muhammad Ali, my boxing hero!

WHAT CAN WE LEARN FROM NATURE'S WISE AND GENTLE GIANTS?

The Never Forgetting Titans

African elephants, nature's gentle giants, embody consistency and reliability in the animal kingdom. These majestic creatures, with their impressive tusks and mighty trunks, are not just built for strength and endurance but also for unwavering determination. In Africa's vast savannas and dense forests, **they face monumental challenges, yet they persevere.**

Elephants' strong family bonds and matriarchal leadership offer valuable lessons in teamwork and dedication. Their herd structure, led by the oldest and wisest female, demonstrates the power of experience and collective wisdom in overcoming obstacles. Their ability to communicate through low-frequency rumbles and body language underscores **the importance of clear, multi-faceted communication in group dynamics.** Combined with their steadfastness, these traits make elephants true champions of the African wilderness.

During long migrations, elephants showcase their extraordinary endurance and problem-solving skills when food and water become scarce. They can travel up to 50 miles a day searching for resources, using their trunks to detect water sources from miles away. Their ability to adapt their foraging habits to changing environments **is a testament to their resourcefulness.** This is a crucial trait in unpredictable and challenging times.

When protecting their young, elephants champion collective care. The entire herd participates in raising calves, with aunts and older siblings often acting as "allomothers." This incredible support system, combined with their strong memory and learned behaviours, helps ensure the survival and success of future generations.

Elephant matriarchs face a unique challenge when guiding their herds through rugged terrain or situations. Leaders must make decisions that affect the entire group's well-being. Nature's solution? Years of accumulated knowledge are passed down through generations.

This wealth of experience and the matriarch's steady guidance help the herd navigate complex challenges and thrive in diverse environments.

In March 2014, Virginia Morrell wrote an article on Science.org discussing how elephants can distinguish our language, age, and threat level by listening to us. It mentions:

- *Elephants possess a sophisticated threat assessment ability, distinguishing between human languages, genders, and ages to gauge danger levels accurately.*

COURAGE

- *Elephant herds demonstrate effective collective learning and knowledge transfer, with older matriarchs passing down crucial survival skills to younger generations.*
- *Elephants exhibit remarkable adaptability by tailoring their responses to specific threats, showcasing context-aware decision-making and behavioural flexibility.[27]*

Mole National Park, in Northern Ghana, is a hotspot for observing its vibrant elephant population. The rangers love their jobs, telling visitors about the park's history and describing the wildlife like proud parents on graduation day. You can walk around the park, escorted by the rangers. My highlight was seeing a herd of elephants enjoying a morning dip in the dam. The matriarch took charge, ensuring the calves washed behind their ears. The bull elephant was a solo trumpet squirting.[28]

How can you Learn from Elephants

Elephants, nature's wise and gentle giants, embody consistency and reliability in the animal kingdom. These majestic creatures, with their impressive tusks and mighty trunks, are not just built for strength and endurance but also for unwavering determination. In Africa's vast savannas and dense forests, **they face monumental challenges, yet they persevere.**

Here are six ways teams can learn from elephants:

1. **Valuing Experience:** Like elephant herds led by wise matriarchs, recognise the value of experienced team members. Their knowledge can guide the team through tough situations and help avoid pitfalls.

2. **Fostering Strong Bonds:** Mimic the elephants' close-knit family structure by promoting strong relationships within your team. This

---

[27] Virginia Morell "Elephants Have Learned to 'Understand Human'" (Science.org 10 Mar 2014) www.science.org/content/article/elephants-have-learned-understand-human

[28] https://molenationalpark.org

Be consistent – dont just keep thinking

creates a supportive environment where members feel secure and valued.

3. **Developing Clear Communication:** Take a leaf from the elephants' book and establish clear, multi-faceted communication channels. This ensures everyone in the team is on the same page and can respond effectively to challenges.

4. **Embracing Collective Problem-Solving:** Just as elephants work together to overcome obstacles, encourage collaborative problem-solving in your team. This approach taps into the collective wisdom and creativity of the group.

5. **Adapting to Change:** Learn from the elephants' ability to adapt their foraging habits in changing environments. Foster a culture of flexibility and resilience in your team to navigate uncertainties.

6. **Nurturing Future Generations**: Like elephants who collectively care for their young, implement mentoring programs where experienced team members guide and support newer ones. This ensures the continuity of knowledge and skills within the team.

COURAGE IN ACTION

As a teenager, I loved watching The Golden Girls. Wednesday nights on Channel 4 were imprinted on my mind, and each episode was a must-see. **The show made significant strides in the television industry by featuring a cast of older women as its protagonists.** Most programs focused on younger characters, and there was hardly anything about older generations, especially women. I watched Betty White, Bea Arthur, Rue McClanahan, and Estelle Getty week after week. Their portrayal of four single women living together in Miami **and their conversations were relatable.** Their pioneering kitchen table chats from four decades earlier made WGBC relatable.

They talked about everyday life. **Topics that everyday people were talking about.** The characters could easily resemble someone's mum, aunt, teacher, neighbour, grandmother **or someone you trust or feel**

comfortable opening up to. All over fifty, these women provided a refreshing and necessary representation of real life. They defied the industry's norms and societal stereotypes.

I envisage Nan inviting her friends to watch my boxing match, sipping hot tea and eating her legendary pie. The tea is served in her posh Royal Doulton cups with matching side plates for the pie. **No social media algorithm matches the reach of this geriatric mafia's chattering and gossip. They tell everyone in their network to build community support.** A homophobe would receive a disapproving look and tongue-lashing from tongues that admonish unpleasantness and reward kindness. The kindness that delivers more tea and apple and blackberry pie.

The Golden Girls resonated with me **because it was funny. Every episode made me laugh.** The show was an ally to the LGBTQ+ community in the 1980s, a time of widespread fear and prejudice. There was rarely any representation of gay characters on television at that time. The Golden Girls featured LGBTQ+ themes and characters with sensitivity and compassion.

It's a reminder **that leadership involves the courage to confront fear and tackle complex issues** head-on, empowering you to make a difference.

Exercise: Allyship and the Dream Pursuit – the Fearless Supporters Challenge

OBJECTIVE: *Develop allyship skills and resilience in pursuing your dreams despite opposition*

This exercise aims to help you strengthen your interpersonal skills by:

1. Recognising the importance of standing up against negativity and bullying.
2. Understanding the value of humour and creativity in addressing challenging situations.

Be consistent – dont just keep thinking

3. Acknowledging the difficulty of pursuing dreams in the face of opposition.
4. Experiencing the satisfaction of educating others and promoting positive behaviour.
5. Learning to guide others while maintaining your own goals and values.
6. Reflecting on personal growth and resilience after facing adversity.
7. This exercise assists in developing empathy, problem-solving skills, and emotional intelligence.

Imaginary Scene

You're Doris, and watching your husband Bert scrolling through social media shows you some nasty comments from trolls about your latest community initiative. You share your concerns over a cuppa with Auntie Maggie (Mrs Thatcher). Auntie Maggie, known for her no-nonsense approach, declares, "They need to go back to school and learn some proper manners." She decides to take action, sending letters to these "temper tantrum adult trolls" instructing them to attend weekend detention.

You and Bert volunteer to supervise the detention, making it a learning experience. As the trolls shuffle in, looking sheepish, you hand out skipping ropes for a fitness test. "Three rounds of two minutes each," you announce cheerfully. The trolls attempt to skip but give up after just 15 seconds, puffing and panting.

Next, you distribute dictionaries. "Right," you say firmly, "Look up the meaning of the words used in your last ten social media posts." One troll nervously raises his hand, whispering, "Mum says I shouldn't use that word."

Bert asks, "What does it mean?"

The red-faced troll mumbles, "It's too rude to say out loud."

COURAGE

You give the troll your famous 'Albert's in trouble' look. Suddenly, Bert lets out a loud fart and quickly blames it on one of the trolls, who cries, "It wasn't me!" You wink at Bert, holding back giggles. Bert quips, "It smelt and tasted like reading your keyboard warrior commentary. Noxious!"

By the end of the detention, the trolls have learned their lesson, fearing the prospect of another letter from Auntie Maggie or attending Bert and Doris' school for naughty Crocs.

Reflection Questions

1. How did you feel about addressing the trolls' behaviour in this creative and humorous way?
2. What role does your experience play in your ability to handle this situation?
3. How might this experience change your approach to future challenges, and what lessons can you draw from it to help others stand up against negativity?

For each of the six pillars of courage, identify a personal memory related to being an ally or pursuing your dreams despite opposition. Reflect on how these memories can help you face future challenges and be a role model for others, much like Doris and Bert were for the trolls.

Scenario 1: Standing Up for a Colleague Facing Discrimination (Example)

Emotional Courage Memory: Sharing personal experiences of overcoming prejudice, creating a safe space for a colleague to express their concerns.

Physical Courage Memory: Physically placing yourself between your colleague and those expressing discriminatory views during a tense meeting.

Moral Courage Memory: Speaking up against discriminatory practices in a high-stakes business negotiation, risking potential deals for integrity.

Be consistent – dont just keep thinking

Empathetic Courage Memory: Actively listening to your colleague's experiences of discrimination without judgment, offering support and validation.

Steadfast Courage Memory: Consistently advocating for inclusive policies over an extended period despite facing resistance from some quarters.

Cerebral Courage Memory: Developing an innovative diversity and inclusion training program for the entire organisation, inspired by your experiences supporting your colleague.

Scenario 2: Pursuing Your Dream Project Despite Scepticism (Your Turn)

Think about a time when you pursued a personal or professional dream despite facing skepticism or opposition. Use the Courage Bank concept to identify memories that can help you stay resilient and supportive of others. Fill in your memories for each type of courage:

Emotional Courage: The willingness to open up to a broad spectrum of emotions.

Memory:

Physical Courage: Acting bravely in the face of fear or pain.

Memory:

Moral Courage: Taking a firm stand for what you believe in and committing to your values.

Memory:

209

COURAGE

Empathetic Courage: Understanding others, practising humility, and setting aside personal bias.

Memory:

Steadfast Courage: Being resolute, focused, and purposeful.

Memory:

Cerebral Courage: Disruption, innovation, and driving change.

Memory:

Remember to approach these questions with honesty and self-compassion. Your development journey is unique, and every step forward, no matter how small, is progress.

WRAP UP

Consistency in action is the key. Instead of hesitating, decide to deliver and get on with it. This mindset was crucial in bringing the World Gay Boxing Championships to life. Every detail and decision, from planning to execution, was a step forward.

Turbulence is temporary, and triumph is usually within reach. You might need help from a friend when changing a lightbulb. They **might steady the stepladder as you climb the steps,** enabling the light to shine.

Courage turns mental mountains into molehills, providing the strength to deliver on your vision.

Be consistent – dont just keep thinking

My three key learnings:

1. Deciding to deliver makes your dream come true and not a future regret.

2. Don't allow anything to dampen your dreams. Enjoy the journey getting to your dream destination

3. Allies make the world a better place.

What are your three learnings?

CHAPTER TWELVE

COURAGE CHAMPION

CHAPTER TWELVE

You're a Brave Courage Champion

HOW COURAGEOUS ARE YOU FEELING?

Courage Champions! A hearty congratulations for making it this far on your journey of bravery. The fact that you're here, reading these words, shows you've already got a fair dinkum amount of courage. Whether you've faced your fears head-on or taken the first step by picking up this book, you've demonstrated the grit and determination that make true courage. So, give yourself a pat on the back – you've earned it!

Now, let's delve into the heart of what we've learned about bravery and how to apply it daily. Remember, courage isn't just for the Boxing Ring; it's for the **Ring of Life.**

So, let's lace up our gloves and get ready to tackle fear with the finesse of a seasoned boxer. *You've already shown you have the potential for courage.*

Now it's time to unleash it in your daily life. You are capable, you are strong, and you are ready!

BARANGAROO'S BRAVE 'FAIR GO' EXAMPLE
Written by my friend Mark Champley

"Many Australians take pride in the term "Fair Go," a phrase that highlights **our nation's commitment to equality and helping each other through tough times.** But where did this term originate? I believe it may be tied to the story of a proud Cameragal woman (her name was Barangaroo) who stood up for fairness in 1791.

When the First Fleet arrived on Gadigal land (Sydney) in 1788, it set off a series of catastrophic events, bringing trauma after trauma to Indigenous communities. The most immediate impact of colonisation was a wave of deadly diseases, including smallpox, measles, and influenza, which decimated communities. Within just fourteen months of the fleet's arrival, Governor Arthur Phillip reported that smallpox had killed half of Sydney's Indigenous population. The sexual abuse of Indigenous girls and women also introduced widespread venereal disease, compounding the suffering.

Amid this upheaval, I was struck by an account from Captain Watkin Tench's journal, "Complete Account of the Settlement at Port Jackson" (London, 1793). In May 1791, a convict was caught stealing fishing gear.

Governor Phillip ordered the convict to be severely flogged in front of as many Aboriginal people as possible to set an example. Forced to watch the punishment, the crowd was horrified. Dar-in-ga wept, and Barangaroo, heavily pregnant, was so enraged that she grabbed a stick and threatened the executioner, demanding an end to the flogging.

Barangaroo's fierce and defiant act, at a time when her people were suffering so greatly, was a powerful statement against unjust punishment. **She stood for fairness, even when it was dangerous to do so.** Tragically, Barangaroo passed away later that year from smallpox, but her legacy endures.

She was laid to rest with her fishing gear – **a symbol of her strength and connection to her culture."**

Her story reminds us that the spirit of a "fair go" runs deep in our history.

WHAT HAVE WE LEARNT: THE NATURE OF COURAGE?

Courage is like a well-trained muscle – it needs consistent exercise to grow strong. Through our journey, we've discovered that bravery isn't a one-size-fits-all trait **but a multifaceted skill we can develop at our own pace.** From emotional vulnerability to physical challenges, from standing up for our values to innovating in the face of adversity, courage takes many forms. This diversity of courage means you can develop it in various aspects of your life, making you more resilient and empowered.

Pace Framework

The PACE framework – **Purpose, Action, Confidence, and Excellence** – is not just a theoretical concept, but a practical and powerful tool for systematically nurturing courage. It underscores that courage starts with a clear purpose, thrives through decisive action, builds confidence through experience, and ultimately leads to excellence through perseverance and continuous improvement. With this framework, you're not just learning about courage; you're equipped to cultivate it in your daily life.

The Six Pillars of Courage

Our exploration of courage has revealed its six pillars: **emotional, physical, moral, empathetic, steadfast, and cerebral.** Each pillar represents a unique aspect of bravery, from opening up to a broad spectrum of emotions to disrupting the status quo with innovative thinking. We've seen how these pillars intertwine, creating a robust framework for facing life's challenges.

Employing Courage as a Habit

To truly embody courage, we must make it a habit in our daily lives. This involves five key steps:

1. **Start from a place of courage** by practising self-care and finding role models;
2. **Lean into Fear** by paying attention to how it manifests and connecting with the truth;
3. **Commit to your values** by doing what's right, not what's easy;

4. **Make courage the norm** by accepting others' journeys and using positive language;

5. and finally, embrace **Be Consistent** by taking action every day, no matter how small.

Remember, courage isn't about sporadic acts of bravery but about cultivating a courageous approach to life. By following these steps and making them part of your daily routine, you'll find that courage becomes less of a conscious effort and more of a natural state of being.

APPLYING YOUR COURAGE KNOWLEDGE

Fear isn't our enemy but a natural part of the human experience we can manage and harness. By taking ownership of our fears, we transform them from roadblocks into steppingstones on our path to growth. Perhaps most importantly, we've discovered that **courage isn't a solitary pursuit.** It thrives in supportive environments and is nurtured by self-care.

The journey to bravery is as much about building resilience within us as it is about fostering connections with others who inspire and uplift us.

Self-Assessment

First, start by giving yourself a **"courage check-up"**. Look at those six pillars of courage and see where you're strong and might need some work. Maybe you're a champion at physical courage but struggle with emotional vulnerability.

We all have our strengths and weaknesses.

Implementing PACE

Next, put the PACE framework into action. Find your purpose – what lights your inner fire? What gets you out of bed in the morning, ready to face the world? Once you've got that sorted, it's time for action. Remember, courage isn't about thinking brave thoughts; it's about doing heroic deeds. Start small if you need to – **but start.**

Building Confidence

As you act, your confidence will grow. **Celebrate those wins, big and small.** Each time you face a fear or overcome an obstacle, you're building your courage muscle. Before you know it, you'll tackle obstacles that once seemed impossible.

Consistency and Self-Care

Don't forget about consistency. **Make courage a daily habit.** It could be as simple as speaking up in a meeting or trying a new food. The key is to keep at it, day in and day out.

Lastly, take care of yourself and surround yourself with a supportive crew. You can't pour from an empty cup, so ensure you look after your physical and mental well-being. And remember, even the toughest boxers have a team in their corner. Find your people – the ones who'll cheer you on and pick you up when you stumble.

5 Tips for Applying Courage in Daily Life

1. Start your day with a courageous intention – choose one small brave act to accomplish.

2. Practice vulnerability – share something personal with a trusted friend or family member.

3. Stand up for your values, even in small ways – it all adds up.

4. Take on a physical challenge that pushes your comfort zone.

5. Regularly reflect on your courage journey – celebrate progress and learn from setbacks.

COURAGE

ONE FINAL COURAGE ADVENTURE

The Future Champion and Upholding Values

The first few weeks of 2024 I spent in Ghana. It included the joyous pleasure of spending time with my good friend **Joshua Quartey**. He is the WGBC African Ambassador and **an outstanding role model for courage and boxing.** He drove me around Bokum, a neighbourhood where boxing is part of the cultural fabric. Kind-hearted people live in the coastal district of Accra. You see **ambitious youth crafting the sweet science in the pugilistic finishing school of Bokum.** The area's network of boxing gyms has produced eight impressive world champions. Spend five minutes in Bokum, and you can see why.

March 2024 brought the decision **to address the persistent issue of homophobia in combat sports.** Despite the existence of Codes of Conduct, high-profile figures were making offensive homophobic slurs with minimal consequences. Frustrated by the lack of enforcement and half-hearted apologies, I spoke out in an interview with The Daily Star, one of the UK's most prominent newspapers.

This was followed by an interview with The Guardian to highlight the progress made in boxing and extend the conversation to MMA. **Taking this stand was risky but necessary.** As the Courage Champion, I felt compelled to speak out against the growing acceptance of intolerance and the blurring of moral lines. If no one challenges this behaviour, it will become the new standard.

By addressing these issues publicly, I aimed to prevent Codes of Conduct from becoming relics of the past.

You miss 100% of the shots you don't take

Nicki – my publicist – suggested we watch a baseball game in Chicago. My excitement glittered. We discovered the Chicago Cubs would play the San Francisco Giants for the Pride Game. What a coincidence! I had this idea:

Wouldn't it be awesome if the Cubs gave WGBC a shoutout? Nicki sent an email and received a lottery jackpot-winning response from the Chicago Cubs. **Would Martin like to throw the ceremonial opening pitch at the Pride Game?**

You miss all the opportunities you don't pursue. One email from my savvy Publicist led to a **once-in-a-lifetime experience.** Here's the kicker: I hadn't thrown a ball since school or even been to a baseball game. I was joining the ranks of Presidents, pop stars, Hollywood actors, prominent sporting personalities, and celebrities. You have probably seen the YouTube videos lampooning ceremonial pitches gone wrong. The ball throw can land in the male proverbials, making him collapse in excruciating and amusing agony.

Sometimes, the invisible hurricane diverts the pitch on a different trajectory and flight path.

Nicky called me with the exciting news at 6 am. My slumber was not awoken by the phone but by the dichotomy of sheer panic and OMG. I sheepishly said, "I don't know how to throw!" and shepherded a weary "Let's do it!". The Courage Champion had a challenge. The chance was too incredible to pass up. I phoned a friend. My Sydney pal, **Professor James Elliott**, is a former professional baseball player for the San Diego Padres and gave me a crash course.

This was also fate. James is from Chicago!

Diva Moment and Community

This trip to America was significant. I stayed with my cousins Ana, Ian, Rebecca, and Kelly, **who are like my siblings.** LinkedIn News asked me to record a video explaining the importance of Pride.

I attended the Compete Sports annual conference in Columbus, Ohio. After speaking with the CEO and leadership team for almost a year, they invited me to join them in Columbus. I met my buddies in the hotel lobby with a round of handshakes that became hugs. They introduced me to the fantastic conference attendees, and I formed instant friendships and became **part of a close-knit community.**

When you're about to do something epic, please make the most of it.

While checking in for my flight to Chicago at Columbus Airport, **I decided to seize the moment and ask if the pilot could give me a shout-out during the flight**. Only a few days to the spotlight! Before boarding, I approached the desk agent, showing a screenshot of the Chicago Cubs press release. She promised to ask the captain. While in my seat, a cabin crew member approached and informed me that it would be up to the captain, but they believed it could happen. He instructed me to start recording when hearing the captain's announcement. Moments later, the captain welcomed everyone on board and said, **"I'd like to welcome Martin Stark, who will be throwing the opening pitch at the Cubs game."** As soon as we landed, the announcement was shared on social media. **I was being a diva.** The social media reactions were a good mixture of ribbing, teasing, congratulatory, teasing, and ribbing.

Windy City Welcome

I love Chicago. There is something about the place that embodies real America with its grit, rugged determination, impressive storytelling architecture, and, best of all, Chicagoans. Proud Chicagoans proudly welcome newcomers to the Windy City.

The Championships were held at a LGBTQ+ boxing gym. Walking into it was like seeing snow or the ocean for the first time. It was more than a gym.

It represented the best of boxing and the LGBTQ+ community, where clients loved spending time.

The ceiling lights emit a sparkling rainbow. The walls have belts, trophies, and posters of champions. The boxing training zone inspires courage and enjoying the sport. The modern equipped gym had excellent trainers and clients who loved training there. It was the venue and the home of the second World Gay Boxing Championships and America's first LGBTQ+ boxing event.

It was also a space to spend time with people you care about

The Ceremonial Opening Pitch

My moment, when one million people watched my pitching prowess, was looming. June 17, 2024, arrived quicker than a fighter jet taking off from London and landing in Paris. A baseball game at **Wrigley Field feels like a Grand Final in Australia.** Nicki and I arrived at the corporate reception, where we were welcomed with open arms. The staff gave me a shirt, "Stark", with the number 22 on the back. They only give these shirts to people throwing the ceremonial opening pitch; what an honour! We were then taken to our seats, the best in the house. I was nervous and excited.

The stadium probably had 12,000 spectators, and over one million people were viewing the game on television or online. **After hearing, "Mr. Stark, it's time to go, " we walked onto the field. I was representing the Stark Clan.** We stepped onto the field, and a staff member handed me the baseball. My name was displayed in bright lights. The announcer said, "Martin, this is your pitch!"

This diva had a plan. Assuming a boxing stance, I executed a bob and weave, and delivered a jab, cross, hook combination. **Oops, that was the wrong sport!** I removed my baseball cap, took the correct stance and tried to remember what James taught me. ***I lobbed the ball, which seemed to veer towards Sydney,*** landing about ten meters to the left of the mascot pitcher. But I didn't care; it landed at the base field, and the crowd erupted in rapturous applause. Nicky congratulated me. **I left Wrigley Field a lifelong Cubs fan. Thanks for the tremendous allyship and opportunity.**

Champions in Chicago

The morning of the Championships began with a relaxing green tea. Depression was lurking, but it would be absent that day. Walking into the gym was the **anticipatory calmness before the majesty of the fireworks lighting up Sydney Harbour** on New Year's Eve. The boxing ring in the middle, the rainbow lights, the spirit, the DJ, the drag queen emcee, fearless fighters, and fab supporters **set the scene for an electric environment and action-packed atmosphere.**

The boxers had a mixture of good butterflies and excitement. They had trained incredibly hard for months. This was their moment, dream, and opportunity. It was an exhibition with no winners or losers; they were all winners.

They represented the best of boxing and exemplified why I love the sport.

The Champions were making the News

There were 50 spectators in the beautiful gym, **the best and most important venue for boxing in 2024.** The DJ and drag queen pumped up the electricity with their brilliance, outperforming any wind farm or meadow of solar panels. The fifty spectators had the energy of the crowd watching the halftime entertainment at the Superbowl.

The standard of boxing was superb. They fought bravely under the supervision of a magnificent referee. They represented the best of boxing and exemplified why I love the sport. It was an exhibition with no winners or losers; they were all winners. **They are champions.**

The Australian Acting Consul-General of Chicago came and showed her support. It was great to have Aussie representation. CBS News arrived to interview me.

They decided to stay the whole day, not moving from their spot for five hours. The final match was reported live.

You're a Brave Courage Champion

Five Fabulous Friends

I made friends with champion allies on LinkedIn five years ago. My face dropped after interviewing two boxers who had finished their fight. Tears welled up seeing five people enter the gym: **Jonaed Iqbal, Susan Leplai Miller, Claudia Wyatt, Future Cain**, and **Sejal Thakkar**. All but Susan had travelled long distances to support me. These are people you have known for years and met in person, and they come to help **you find your purpose, dream, and passion in life. Thanks, champs!**

Exiting the ring, I hugged Claudia. She just listened. There were hugs from all my special friends, thanking them for everything and for being there through the past five years when I was grappling with depression, supporting the Chicago and Sydney events. It felt like the Olympics were starting in Chicago at the gym.

It showcased what the sport of boxing can achieve and what everyone in the room contributed to this significant milestone, this triumph.

WRAP UP AND CLOSE

The challenges, comas, and tracheotomy did not stop me. Addison's disease has not stopped me. For too many years, I moved forward with part-time confidence and resilience.

Owning and disrupting the fear makes you take more confident strides, swimming in the ocean of abundant resilience.

Nothing can change what you have achieved. Courage can make your success more outstanding and accessible.

I end this book by asking you, when will you next be courageous?

From a Fan

Courage – welcome to the only book you'll ever need to revolutionise your life, your business, your team with a unique and always entertaining approach.

Martin Stark gives you the tools and the insight that will change the way you look at life forever.

Using clever analogies drawn from our animal Kingdom, Martin takes you on a journey you won't forget.

Unputdownable, Courage is the life and business playbook you didn't know you needed until now.

Watch with wonder as he explores beastly beatitudes and creates a highway to success and happiness on all levels.

Inspirational? Totally.

Aspirational? That too.

Genius? Probably– at least I think so.

Chris Matheson-Green

Synopsis

"Courage: Your Right Hook" by Martin Stark is a powerful exploration of bravery. As a gay man who has faced life-threatening illnesses, Stark offers a unique perspective on courage. He breaks it down into six fundamental pillars: emotional, physical, moral, empathetic, steadfast, and cerebral, and provides the steps to make courage a habit.

This book is more than a recount of Stark's journey from hospital beds to founding the World Gay Boxing Championships. It's a hands-on guide that empowers readers to integrate courage into their daily lives, introducing the PACE framework (Purpose, Action, Confidence, Excellence) for cultivating and sustaining courage.

Stark demonstrates courage through personal stories, historical references, and natural examples. Each chapter offers actionable strategies for readers to apply in their own lives. This book is more than a memoir or self-help book; it's a potent catalyst for personal transformation. Stark challenges readers to embrace vulnerability, stand firm in their values, and practice courage daily.

Connect with Martin Stark for more insights and practical tips on building courage:

Visit his website **https://martinstark.co**

Subscribe to his Courage Bytes newsletter:
https://couragebytes.substack.com/

Follow his professional journey on LinkedIn at
https://www.linkedin.com/in/martin-stark-au/

Watch inspiring content on YouTube
https://www.youtube.com/@TheCourageChampion

"Courage: Your Right Hook" by Martin Stark is a powerful exploration of bravery in its many forms. As a gay man who has faced life-threatening illnesses, including comas and Addison's disease, Stark offers a unique perspective on courage. He breaks it down into six fundamental pillars: emotional, physical, moral, empathetic, steadfast, and cerebral, and provides the steps to make courage a habit.

This book is more than just a recount of Stark's journey from hospital beds to founding the World Gay Boxing Championships. It's a hands-on guide that empowers readers to integrate courage into their daily lives. Stark introduces the PACE framework (Purpose, Action, Confidence, Excellence), a practical tool for cultivating and sustaining courage.

Stark illustrates how courage manifests in various situations Through personal anecdotes, historical examples, and insights from nature. From standing up against discrimination to persevering through physical challenges, each chapter offers actionable strategies for readers to apply in their own lives.

"Courage: Your Right Hook" is more than a memoir or self-help book; it's a potent catalyst for personal transformation. Stark challenges readers to embrace vulnerability, stand firm in their values, and practice courage daily.

This inspiring book equips readers with strategies to confront personal, professional, and societal challenges, inspiring them to lead a more authentic, courageous life.

ISBN 978-1-7637398

9 781763 739817

www.ingramcontent.com/pod-product-compliance
Lightning Source LLC
Chambersburg PA
CBHW050859160426
43194CB00011B/2210